FROM BARELY SURVIVING TO THRIVING

Purpose Letters Vol 3 | A 30-Day Devotional

Dr. Samuel Ekundayo

FROM BARELY SURVIVING TO THRIVING

Copyright© 2025 | Dr Samuel Ekundayo

All rights reserved; no part of this publication may be reproduced, stored in a retrieval system or transmitted in any form or by any means electrical, mechanical, photocopying, recording or otherwise – without the prior written permission of the author or publisher.

The right of Dr Samuel Ekundayo to be identified as the author of this book has been asserted by him in accordance with copyright laws.

ISBN: 978-1-7385992-5-7

For all information, address all correspondence to the author's website: www.samuelekundayo.com

DEDICATION

This book is dedicated to you dear reader. I pray that you will discover and fulfil the purpose of God for your life and be all He has created you to be in Jesus' name.
Amen!

I believe in you.

ACKNOWLEDGEMENTS

Firstly, I thank God for giving me the ability to write this book. Every opportunity to bless my generation through my writing give me so much fulfilment and I attribute that to the grace and gift of God.

To my Dudushewa and Treasure, I thank you for your consistent love, encouragement, and companionship. Thank you for believing in me and always rooting for me. I love you endlessly.

And to my parents (biological and spiritual), mentors and guides God has placed over me, thank you for all you have done and still doing to stir me in the right direction. I will always be grateful.

Special thanks to my team of amazing and God-sent individuals God has used for me to write this book. Pastor Ayodele Mike for your help in rewriting the initial parts of the book; Pastor Sam Adetiran for helping me edit the book, and my beloved Opeoluwa Adebakin for the beautifully designed book cover.

Table of Contents

DEDICATION 3

ACKNOWLEDGEMENTS 4

Day 1 DEVELOP AN ANTI-MAJORITY MINDSET! 7

Day 2 THE DANGER OF A FIXED MINDSET 14

Day 3 DO YOU WRITE DOWN YOUR GOALS? 21

Day 4 AVAILABILITY OVER ABILITY 28

Day 5 BUILT FOR DOMINION 35

Day 6 EXCELLENCE IS A SEED 42

Day 7 OBSCURITY IS NOT ALWAYS A CURSE 49

Day 8 MAKE THE MOST OF TIME 56

Day 9 DOING MORE WITH LESS 63

Day 10 GET TO WORK 70

Day 11 BENEFITS OF CONSISTENCY! 76

Day 12 POWER OF ACCESS TO THE RIGHT PEOPLE 83

Day 13 LIVE FOR SOMETHING! 90

Day 14 THE VOICES IN YOUR LIFE 97

Day 15 YOU ARE NOT YOUR BODY 104

Day 16 HOW TO BEGIN TO ENJOY PRAYER 111

Day 17 YOU ARE THE LIGHT OF THE WORLD! 118

Day 18 THERE IS MORE TO YOU 124

Day 19 QUIT TALKING, START WORKING 130

Day 20 CREATED TO BE A BLESSING 136

Day 21 A LITTLE BIT MORE 143

Day 22 NOBODY HAS A PERFECT LIFE 149

Day 23 GO FOR IT! 155

Day 24 DONT LOSE EVERYTHING!!! 160

Day 25 PRAY BUT ALSO WORK! 167

Day 26 YOU MUST KNOW WHAT YOU DONT KNOW 174

Day 27 WHAT IS YOUR GOAL? 181

Day 28 WHY PEOPLE MAKE THE WRONG DECISIONS . 186

Day 29 COME OUT AND STEP OUT 192

Day 30 YOU CAN MAKE A DIFFERENCE 197

Day 1
DEVELOP AN ANTI-MAJORITY MINDSET!

The first requirement for living an extraordinary life, even in the most difficult seasons, is not about doing miraculous or supernatural things. It's about doing the ordinary in an extraordinary way. That's right—your breakthrough is often hidden in your ability to show up faithfully, consistently, and excellently in what others overlook.

There's a scripture that often gets quoted, and rightly so, because it reveals this very principle: *"Then Isaac sowed in that land, and received in the same year a hundredfold: and the Lord blessed him. And the man waxed great, and went forward, and grew until he became very great."* (Genesis 26:12–13). For a long time, I believed Isaac must have done something remarkable or prophetic to get such a miraculous return in the time of famine. But recently, the Lord opened my eyes to something deeper. Isaac didn't do something extraordinary—he simply *sowed*. He did what was *ordinary*, but he did it in a time and way that no one else was willing to.

Extraordinary people often ask themselves one vital question: *What is the opportunity in this situation?* While the majority complain, retreat, or merely endure, extraordinary people invest. They think forward. They act in faith. They do what others aren't willing to do—not because they have more resources, but because they have a different mindset.

You don't need to be multi-talented or supernaturally gifted to live this way. Doing the ordinary in an extraordinary way doesn't require ten spiritual gifts or a global platform. It requires intention. Think of two employees with the same role. One simply fulfils the job description; the other tidies up the office, arranges files, goes the extra mile. They both do the same job, but the second person sets themselves apart—not by doing something new, but by doing something *better*.

Isaac had what I call an anti-majority mindset. He did what others wouldn't. He didn't follow the victim mentality. He didn't wait for better circumstances. He sowed in the land—even in famine. And in that same year, he reaped a hundredfold. It wasn't the seed that was extraordinary. It was his mindset.

When others were saying, "Why waste seed in a dry land?" Isaac was planting. When the average person was preserving the little they had just to survive another day, Isaac was *investing* in a harvest he could not yet see. He didn't eat his seed—he sowed it.

This is a powerful lesson. Don't eat your seed just because the environment looks unfavourable. Don't follow the masses, even when their reasoning makes sense. Faith is not always logical, but it's always fruitful. Many people miss their breakthrough not because they lack the seed, but because they lack the *faith to sow* it.

You must be willing to go the extra mile—to sow when others are retreating. It may not be comfortable, and it may not be popular, but it is the way of increase. God honours faith-driven obedience.

The principle of sowing goes beyond finances. It's about sowing time, energy, commitment, excellence, and prayer into the things God has laid on your heart. Isaac didn't wait for others to plant. He didn't wait for collective consensus. He didn't seek permission from the majority. He acted in faith.

The real difference between high-flyers and the average person is what they *see*. Isaac saw a future worth investing in. He believed in a harvest that others couldn't imagine. There are people today who refuse to make sacrifices because they don't believe in a better tomorrow. But if you can see what

God sees, you'll do what others won't. And if you do what others won't, you'll experience what others never will.

The future isn't far off—it's right in front of you. The future you prayed about yesterday is the reality you're living in today. And the ones enjoying today are those who sowed diligently yesterday. While others are merely enduring this season, those who invested earlier are reaping joyfully.

Even in your country—regardless of economic conditions—there are people building, launching, expanding, and thriving. Don't get caught in the trap of complaining about your environment. Your economy is not your source—*God is.* While others cry and blame systems, you can rise and sow into your calling.

When everyone else was focused on surviving, Isaac was focused on sowing. When people were blaming God or hoarding their last resources, Isaac was walking the fields with seed in his hands. He dared to trust that something planted in famine could still produce a harvest.

This is your moment to ask: What am I doing in this season? Am I sowing into my future? Am I investing in my growth, my calling, my spiritual maturity? Or am I sitting on my seed, hoping for change but too afraid to act?

You must break free from the crowd. The majority rarely experiences greatness because the majority often chooses comfort. You weren't called to blend in. You were called to stand out—to operate by faith, not fear. And faith is never passive; faith moves. Faith acts. Faith sows.

This is not the season to coast. It's not the season to delay. The earlier you sow, the sooner you reap. Don't wait for validation. Don't wait for ideal conditions. Remember Ecclesiastes 11:4: *"Whoever watches the wind will not plant; whoever looks at the clouds will not reap."*

Stop waiting. Start sowing. Your future will thank you.

You have what it takes to do what the majority will not do. You have seed. You have faith. And you have a God who promises to bless your obedience.

So the question remains: In this difficult season, are you sowing? Or are you just trying to survive?

Choose to be different. Choose to invest in your future. Choose to sow your seed, even when it doesn't make sense.

I believe in you.

Day 2
THE DANGER OF A FIXED MINDSET

One of the greatest dangers in life is not failure—it's having a **fixed mindset**. A fixed mindset will keep you stuck in the same place for years, while others move forward, experiencing breakthrough, healing, and progress. Jesus could be passing by—healing others, opening doors, doing the miraculous—and yet you might miss out. Why? Because you were only expecting Him to come through in the *same way He did before*.

You assume, "Because God healed me through a doctor in 2001, He must do it the same way again." Or "Since the last breakthrough came through a particular connection, it must come that way again." But friend, that's not how God works.

You may even use Scripture to justify this thinking—*"Jesus Christ is the same yesterday, today, and forever"* (Hebrews 13:8). That verse speaks of His *character*, not His *methods*. Yes, His nature is consistent—He is always loving, faithful, powerful, and true. But His **methods are diverse**. He is the God of variety, the One who parted the Red Sea *for Moses*, but chose to stop the Jordan River *for Joshua*. Same God. Different approach.

One of the fascinating things about Jesus' earthly ministry is that He almost never performed a miracle the same way twice. To heal one blind man, He spoke a word. For another, He spat on the ground, made mud, and rubbed it on his eyes (John 9:6). Why? He was teaching us not to box Him in. God is sovereign—He does what He wills, when He wills, and *how* He wills. You cannot confine an infinite God to your finite expectations.

God resists being put into a formula. And yet, that's exactly what a fixed mindset tries to do. It assumes, "God must act like this, or He's not acting at all." But the Lord says in Isaiah 55:8–9, *"For My thoughts are not your thoughts, neither are your ways My ways ... as the heavens are higher than the earth, so are My ways higher than your ways and My thoughts than your thoughts."* His ways transcend our understanding.

To walk with God effectively, you must *expand your thinking*. The Kingdom of God does not operate within the narrow confines of man-made traditions. It flows with divine creativity and supernatural wisdom.

The danger of a fixed mindset is that it convinces you that "this is just how things are." You stop expecting newness. You stop believing for more. You become too familiar with your routine, your limitations, and even your pain. A fixed mindset keeps you *caged*, even when the door is wide open.

And here's the irony: while we may not be able to operate on God's level, we *are* created to think like Him. Psalm 82:6 says, *"I said, 'You are gods, and all of you are children of the Most High.'"* This doesn't mean we are divine beings, but it does mean we've been made in His image, empowered with His Spirit, and invited to reflect His nature and mindset. A mindset of **possibility.**

You are not stuck—unless you think you are. You are not small—unless you believe you are. The limitations we experience often begin in the mind. Proverbs 23:7 says, *"As a man thinks in his heart, so is he."* That's why Satan attacks your mindset. He doesn't need chains to hold you—he just needs your agreement with limitation.

A fixed mindset says, *"This is the only way it can happen."* But God says, *"Behold, I will do a new thing; now it shall spring forth, shall you not know it?"* (Isaiah 43:19). God is in the business of new things. He thrives in creativity. But if your mind is stuck in the old, you will miss the new.

God is not a traditionalist. He doesn't need to fit into your system, your background, your denomination, or your expectations. He simply asks for your trust.

God wants to stretch you. He wants to take you beyond routine and normalcy. He wants to open your eyes to divine possibilities. But He can only take you as far as your mindset will allow. *"According to your faith be it unto you"* (Matthew 9:29). If your faith is restricted by tradition and predictability, your experience of God's power will be limited.

Many people live on autopilot—stuck in the same daily patterns, emotionally dry, spiritually stagnant, creatively numb. They say they want more, but their mindset says otherwise. The fixed mind makes you comfortable with mediocrity and allergic to risk. It says, *"Let's play it safe,"* while God is saying, *"Step out on the water."*

Jesus didn't call Peter to walk on water because it was rational. He called him because it was *divine.* And Peter only sank when he took his eyes off Jesus and focused on his surroundings (Matthew 14:29–30). In the same way, you will only sink into limitation when you focus on the natural instead of the supernatural possibilities of God.

And here's the clincher: **God is always willing to do more, but He won't force it.** He wants to express His creativity through you, but He will only move to the degree you allow Him. If your heart says, *"I don't think God can use me,"* He won't override your will. But if your heart says, *"Be it unto me according to Your Word,"* then get ready to be blown away.

A fixed mindset is not just a mental block—it's a spiritual hindrance. It can blind you to divine instruction, make you resistant to growth, and rob you of encounters meant to elevate you. The longer you cling to what you've always known, the more you forfeit the fresh oil God wants to pour.

This is your moment to break the box.

Don't let your mind be a prison. Be willing to think beyond the familiar. Be open to God doing something *you've never seen before*. He is not asking you to figure it out; He's asking you to *trust Him enough* to let go of your limited view and embrace His supernatural ways.

There's more. So much more. But the level you experience is tied to the level you're willing to believe.

God is not done with you. He's only just beginning. So ditch the fixed mindset. Be flexible. Be expectant. Be bold.

Because when you finally let go of the old ways of thinking, you make room for the *new things* God is longing to do in your life.

You were never meant to be predictable—you were created to be powerful.

Get ready. God is about to amaze you.

Day 3
DO YOU WRITE DOWN YOUR GOALS?

Goals are powerful. They give direction, clarity, and focus. But as important as goals are, they become far more potent when they are *written down*. A goal that is not written is merely a wish, a fleeting desire without accountability or structure.

As believers, it is vital that we set goals not just for personal success, but for fulfilling God's divine purpose in our lives. Without goals—especially goals aligned with God's purpose—you will always struggle to achieve the very things heaven has already assigned to you.

One major reason many people don't set goals is the fear of failure. The moment they pick up a pen to write something down, it suddenly feels like a binding commitment they might not live up to. And instead of being motivated, they become overwhelmed. But let's be honest—it's not failure itself that hinders people, it's the *fear* of it.

The fear of failure has crippled many destinies. It has silenced potential authors, buried inventions, paused ministries, and delayed businesses. And yet, fear has no hands, no feet, no voice—only the power you give it. It is one of Satan's most effective tools to paralyze God's children.

"God has not given us a spirit of fear, but of power and of love and of a sound mind" (2 Timothy 1:7). Fear is not from God. Courage is.

When you allow fear to stop you from pursuing your goals, you are essentially allowing the enemy to rob you of your divine assignment. But when you rise above fear and write those goals down—boldly and prayerfully—you are planting seeds for God to water with grace, wisdom, and provision.

Let me tell you something profound: Your goals are not just about you. Achieving your goals gives glory to God. Every fulfilled purpose, every goal met, every dream realised becomes a testimony of God's power working in and through you. It builds your confidence, strengthens your faith, and becomes a platform for others to believe God for more.

That's why I urge you: don't just *have* goals—*commit* to them by writing them down. It's a spiritual discipline. God told the prophet Habakkuk, *"Write the vision and make it plain on tablets, that he may run who reads it"* (Habakkuk 2:2). Vision becomes actionable when it is written. Clarity is born when pen meets paper.

But don't stop at writing vague ideas. Make your goals SMART.

SMART stands for:

- **Specific** – What exactly do you want to accomplish? Avoid vague goals like "I want to be successful" or "I want to be more spiritual." Be clear. For example, "I want to read the New Testament in 90 days" or "I want to launch my podcast by September."
- **Measurable** – How will you know you've achieved it? Create markers of progress. Without a way to track it, you won't know when to celebrate.
- **Attainable** – Faith doesn't mean being unrealistic. We serve a God of miracles, yes, but we also walk with wisdom. Set goals you can reach by God's grace and your discipline.
- **Relevant and Realistic** – Is the goal aligned with your calling? Does it matter in the light of eternity and purpose?
- **Time-bound** – Set a deadline. Open-ended goals rarely get done. Time frames fuel urgency and discipline.

Let's say it's January 1st and you set a goal to write and publish your book, *"The Power of Everyday,"* by December 31st. Here's how to make it SMART:

Goal: Write and publish *The Power of Everyday* by 31st December.

Action Plan:

- Finish the outline by January 15th.
- Write one chapter per week for 8 weeks—complete manuscript by March 20th.
- Research publishers between March 21st and 30th.
- Choose a publisher by April 10th.
- Save $100 per week toward publishing expenses or speak to one person weekly for potential sponsorship.

The more detailed your plan, the greater your chances of success. You remove confusion, increase focus, and build momentum. It's no longer a dream—it becomes a structured journey.

This is not theory. This works. I've seen it firsthand in my life. It's one of my greatest personal secrets to productivity, achievement, and fulfilment. When I write down my goals, things shift. Ideas come. Divine connections appear.

Resources align. And the more I act on them, the more God multiplies my efforts.

Friend, your goals are real, and they are possible. They are tied to God's will for your life. If you don't rise to achieve them, someone else might, because heaven's agenda will not go unfulfilled. But wouldn't it be better if *you* fulfilled the assignment God gave *you*?

So take this seriously. Write down your goals. Don't keep them in your head. Get a goal journal or notebook—something sacred to capture your destiny in motion. Be addicted to writing goals. Be serious. Be focused. Be prayerful.

And don't stop at writing—*speak* about your goals. The more you talk about them, the more they take root in your heart. Faith comes by hearing (Romans 10:17), and that includes hearing your own voice affirm your mission.

Pray over your goals. Present them before God. Ask Him for grace, wisdom, and divine help. Proverbs 16:3 says, *"Commit your work to the Lord, and your plans will be established."* You're not doing this alone. God is with you every step of the way.

If you're unsure where to begin, write anyway. Start somewhere. You can refine your goals as clarity comes. And if you'd like guidance, I'm happy to help. Write out your goals, send them my way, and I'd be honoured to give feedback.

Let me leave you with this sobering thought: *If you have no goals, you have no right to succeed.* Success is not accidental—it is intentional. And intention without direction is chaos. God doesn't bless laziness or confusion. He blesses purpose, vision, and movement.

So get up now. Write something. Start small if you must—but start. You'll be amazed at how much you can achieve when your heart, mind, pen, and prayers align.

God bless you as you write the vision and run with it.

Day 4
AVAILABILITY OVER ABILITY

Some years ago, I went to a local shop near my house to buy something. When I got there, the place was closed. Curious, I checked the sign on the door which clearly stated their opening time—9:30am. I glanced at my watch. It was 9:34am. Just a few minutes late, I thought, so I waited. I even called the number displayed on their door, but no one answered. I continued to wait—9:42am—and still, no one showed up. Disappointed, I turned back to my car and left.

As I sat in my car reflecting on the experience, one powerful truth hit me like lightning: **Ability without availability is useless.**

That shop may have had great products. The owners may have been skilled and experienced. But none of that mattered when they were unavailable. Their ability to serve didn't benefit anyone that morning because they simply weren't there. And isn't that a reflection of how many of us are with God?

God is not seeking the most powerful, the most skilled, or the most qualified. He is seeking the *available*. The ones who show up. The ones who say, "Here I am, Lord, send me" (Isaiah 6:8). Throughout Scripture, God consistently chooses people not based on their ability, but their availability.

Take David for example. He wasn't the most obvious choice to take on Goliath. He was a shepherd, not a soldier. But he was available. When others were paralyzed by fear, David stepped forward. He didn't show up with a sword or a shield, but with trust in God and a sling in his hand—and God used him mightily (1 Samuel 17).

Or consider Moses. When God called him at the burning bush, Moses was full of excuses: "I am not eloquent," "I am slow of speech," "Send someone else" (Exodus 4:10-13). But despite his hesitation and perceived inadequacies, Moses made himself available. And that simple act of availability led to the deliverance of an entire nation.

The Bible is full of such examples. God is not looking for perfection—He's looking for permission. He's not looking for superheroes—He's looking for surrendered vessels. In fact, the more broken, inadequate, and ordinary the vessel, the more the glory of God is seen when He moves through them.

God specializes in using:

- The weak but willing
- The unsure but surrendered
- The overlooked but obedient

- The broken but believing
- The disqualified by men but chosen by Heaven

It's not about your résumé; it's about your readiness.

Remember 1 Samuel 2:9: *"For by strength shall no man prevail."* This verse couldn't be clearer—our strength, talents, and natural capabilities have their limits. They are not what qualifies us for divine assignment. In fact, reliance on our own strength is often what disqualifies us. God doesn't want your power—He wants your posture. A posture of humility, obedience, and availability.

Paul echoes this in 2 Corinthians 12:9 where God says, *"My grace is sufficient for you, for My strength is made perfect in weakness."* Think about that. God's strength is not perfected in your strength—it is perfected in your weakness. When you acknowledge that you're not enough on your own, but you're available for God to use, He steps in and fills the gap with His glory.

Sometimes, we disqualify ourselves from being used by God because we don't feel worthy. We look at our flaws, our sins, our limitations, and we think, *"God can't use someone like me."* But that's a lie from the enemy. If God only used the qualified, no one would be used.

- Noah got drunk.
- Abraham lied.
- Jacob was a deceiver.
- Rahab was a prostitute.
- Jonah ran from God.
- Peter denied Jesus.
- Paul persecuted Christians.

Yet, all these people made themselves available, and God used them to do the extraordinary. The truth is, God can't do much with a person who is full of themselves, but He can do wonders through someone who is empty and yielded.

Let me ask you: are you available? Not *perfect*, not *ready*, not *polished*—just available.

Sometimes, we're too busy for God. Too caught up in the hustle. Too preoccupied with building our own kingdoms to serve in His. We wake up, scroll, hustle, plan, post, work—and yet never ask, *"Lord, what would You have me do today?"*

God is still looking for men and women who will say yes. He's still recruiting vessels—not because He needs help, but because He delights in partnership. He could have sent angels to spread the gospel, but He chose us instead. Not because we're impressive, but because we're image-bearers with a divine mandate.

And here's the reward: when you make yourself available to God, your life cannot remain ordinary. It is *impossible* to stay the same when you walk with God. Moses went up the mountain and came down glowing. Isaiah had one encounter with God and went from *"Woe is me"* to *"Send me."* Peter denied Jesus three times, but when he was filled with the Holy Spirit, he preached one sermon and 3,000 were saved.

Availability positions you for transformation. And not just personal transformation—but impact, fruitfulness, and eternal significance.

So if you're wondering why your life feels stuck, why there's no momentum, no progress—ask yourself honestly: *"Am I truly available to God?"* Or am I making excuses? Am I telling God, "Use me later," "Use me when I'm ready," "Use me after I've got it all together"?

If you're not making yourself available, don't be surprised that you're not being used. But the moment you shift from *ability-focused* to *availability-focused*, everything begins to change.

This is your wake-up call. God is not looking for your skill, your status, or your strength. He's looking for your surrender. The greatest ability in the Kingdom is *availability*.

Are you available?

Are you ready to be inconvenienced for the sake of His calling?

Are you willing to say, "Yes Lord," even when you don't know the full plan?

God doesn't need you to be a superhero. He just needs you to be there.

I believe in you.

Day 5
BUILT FOR DOMINION

You were not built for survival; you were built for dominion. That may sound countercultural, especially in a world saturated with competition, self-preservation, and comparison. But it's the truth of your design. One theory I've always found fundamentally flawed is Charles Darwin's "Survival of the Fittest," which stems from the evolutionary theory of natural selection. While it may describe the animal kingdom, it fails miserably when applied to mankind.

You see, evolutionary theory essentially reduces humanity to mere participants in a chaotic struggle for life—a fight to prove who is strongest, smartest, or most adaptable. But man is not an accident of evolution. We are the intentional creation of a sovereign God, made in His image and likeness (Genesis 1:26). We were never designed to *survive* like wild animals; we were designed to *reign* like kings.

In the animal kingdom, maybe there are superior species. But among men, we are all favoured by God. The issue isn't about *who* is favoured; it's about *who knows it*. Those who appear to be ahead are not more special than you. They are simply individuals who have awakened to their dominion mandate and are walking boldly in it.

We are not locked in a life-or-death struggle with each other. The Kingdom of God is not a battleground of believers striving to outdo one another—it is a realm of kings, each reigning within his or her God-ordained domain. When we understand this, we stop seeing each other as threats and start functioning as co-labourers in God's expansive vineyard.

Let's define this properly: two things make a king—**territory** and **authority**. A king without territory has no throne to rule from, and a king without authority is merely a figurehead. Your God-given kingship requires both. And here lies the problem: many people haven't discovered their territory yet. That's why they hustle. That's why they strive, stress, and compete endlessly—because they haven't stepped into their divine domain.

Hustlers may work hard, but they often lack clarity. They are like slaves running aimlessly, reacting to life rather than ruling over it. But God didn't call you to hustle—He called you to *dominate*. He said, *"Be fruitful and multiply; fill the earth and subdue it; have dominion..."* (Genesis 1:28). That's not survival language. That's kingdom language.

The moment you discover your place—your unique calling, assignment, and sphere of influence—you will begin to operate with authority. You won't have to strive to be seen or heard. You won't need to fight to prove your worth. Why? Because *kings don't hustle—they reign.*

Jesus put it this way in John 8:32: *"You shall know the truth, and the truth shall make you free."* When you discover the truth of your dominion mandate, it sets you free from every peasant mindset. You stop seeing life as a battlefield for survival and start seeing it as a field for fruitful stewardship.

Most of the struggles people face today can be traced back to this single issue: they are operating outside their territory. When you function outside your God-ordained domain, everything feels like war. But once you discover your lane, you find grace, ease, and authority.

In your territory, you're unbeatable. Not because you're better than others, but because that's the domain God designed *you* for. It's your Eden—your place of stewardship, cultivation, and dominion. God placed Adam *in* the Garden, not just *on* the earth. Likewise, He has a specific place, purpose, and platform for you.

Unfortunately, many lose sight of their domain and begin to envy the domains of others. And here's the danger: envy is a sign of disconnection from purpose. When you know who you are and where you belong, envy dies. It has no room to breathe in a heart full of purpose. But when your eyes are fixed on someone else's lane, you'll always feel like you're falling behind—even when you're not called to run that race.

Envy is simply misplaced focus. And misdirected focus always breeds frustration. But once you rediscover your territory, your admiration turns into inspiration—not jealousy. You no longer try to copy others; instead, you rise to take full ownership of your unique assignment.

Listen carefully: the sky is wide enough for every bird to fly. They don't collide, not because the sky is small, but because each bird understands how to spread its wings and soar in its own lane. So it is with the Kingdom of God. Your wings were never meant to clash with someone else's. They were meant to expand, to soar, to fill the earth with your unique contribution.

This is not a call to comparison—it's a call to dominion. It's time to stop striving to be everything to everyone and start reigning as the king in your own domain. Your assignment was never meant to compete; it was meant to complement the tapestry of the Kingdom.

You were not created to blend in or compete endlessly for attention. You were created to *stand out* by fulfilling your God-given assignment with clarity and excellence. Romans 12:6 tells us, *"Having then gifts differing according to the grace that is given to us, let us use them."* That's your lane. That's your domain. Use it.

So, what does it take to truly walk in dominion?

It starts with discovery—ask God to reveal your territory. Then comes discipline—cultivate that territory with diligence.
Followed by distinction—stand in your authority and represent Jesus boldly. And finally, destiny—when you live out your assignment, you fulfil your divine purpose on the earth.

The world doesn't need more hustlers. It needs more kings—more purpose-driven individuals who know who they are, where they belong, and what they've been called to do.

So rise up. Stop shrinking to fit survival mode when you were built to dominate. Stop apologising for your calling. Stop envying what's not yours. Step into your domain with confidence, knowing that what God has assigned to you, *only you* can fulfil.

You have a domain. You are a king. You were not created to survive—you were created to reign.

I believe in you.

Day 6
EXCELLENCE IS A SEED

Some time ago, I went to get my hair cut. I had discovered a barber not too far from my house—a skilled gentleman whose craft impressed me from our very first encounter. Since then, I'd kept going back, not because of his personality or proximity, but because of the excellence with which he did his job.

I remember one particular day I sat in his chair, and he was trying so hard to engage me in a conversation. You could tell he was working on his customer service skills—chatting me up, asking questions, and trying to get to know me. But I could feel the effort. It wasn't flowing naturally.

And I thought to myself, *"Don't worry about the small talk. What keeps me coming back isn't your conversation—it's the excellence in your work."*

That moment taught me something profound, and I want to share it with you.

The truth is, people are drawn to excellence. Whether it's in ministry, business, creativity, or service, what makes others invite you, follow you, buy from you, or trust you with opportunities often has less to do with how loud your voice is and more to do with how excellent your work is.

Excellence is magnetic. It pulls people toward you. Proverbs 22:29 says, *"Do you see a man skilled in his work? He will stand before kings; he will not stand before obscure men."* This isn't just a proverb—it's a principle of the Kingdom. Skill and excellence position you before greatness. Excellence opens doors that charisma alone cannot.

Let's be honest: you can try to polish your personality, master public speaking, and post consistently on social media—but if your gift is not sharpened and refined, those efforts may only go so far. Excellence is what makes your gift memorable and impactful.

Think about it: could you imagine Jesus performing His earthly ministry half-heartedly? Could you picture Him healing someone lazily or teaching the multitudes unprepared? Never. Every miracle, every parable, every conversation was laced with divine precision and compassion. He even made sure leftovers were gathered after feeding the five thousand (John 6:12)—that's intentionality.

Why? Because excellence reflects the nature of God.

Colossians 3:23 tells us, *"Whatever you do, work at it with all your heart, as working for the Lord, not for human masters."* That means mediocrity isn't even an option for a child of God. We represent a King, and we must live like ambassadors of Heaven. Excellence is part of our divine identity.

Look at creation. The skies don't just exist—they declare the glory of God (Psalm 19:1). The human body isn't merely functional—it's intricately and wonderfully made (Psalm 139:14). From the stars in the galaxies to the cells in your body, everything God made bears the mark of intentionality and brilliance.

You were made in His image (Genesis 1:27), and He expects you to mirror His excellence in how you steward your calling. Whether you are a teacher, pastor, designer, engineer, singer, parent, or entrepreneur—your work should reflect the excellence of your Creator.

You're probably saying, *"But I'm not perfect."* And I agree—none of us are. We're human. But excellence isn't about perfection; it's about *intentionality and diligence.* It's about giving your best, refining your skill, showing up prepared, and never settling for less than what you're capable of.

If you're a chef, people can taste the effort. If you're a writer, people can read the passion. If you're a speaker, people can feel the weight of preparation. If you're a leader, people can trust your consistency.

Even God celebrates diligence. Proverbs 13:4 says, *"The soul of the diligent shall be made rich."* That richness is not only financial—it includes favour, reputation, fulfilment, and influence.

Let me be real with you: excellence takes effort. You won't stumble into greatness casually. It takes time, study, training, and constant refinement. But that's what makes it worth it.

When I'm invited to speak—even if it's to just two people—I give my 150%. Why? Because those two people deserve my best. Because God deserves my best. Because I understand that the seed of excellence I plant in a small room will eventually bear fruit in greater spaces.

Don't wait until the platform is grand to become excellent. Excellence is not for the stage—it's for your stewardship. David didn't become a giant slayer when he faced Goliath—he had already been practicing with lions and bears in the secret place (1 Samuel 17:34-37).

Let me ask you again: *Are you excellent at what you do—or are you just getting by?* Are you doing the bare minimum, or are you pushing for mastery? Are you trying to impress, or are you truly adding value?

Excellence is not in the spotlight—it's in the secret place. It's in the late nights of learning, the humble hours of practice, the quiet moments of prayerful preparation. It's in the diligence of showing up even when no one claps.

Excellence doesn't scream; it echoes. Long after the show is over, long after the conversation ends, people remember how you made them feel—and how well you served them.

As a believer, your work is your worship. Romans 12:1 calls us to present our lives as *"a living sacrifice, holy and acceptable to God—which is your spiritual worship."* That includes how you run your business, teach your students, write your book, style your client, or design your product. Every act of excellence is a fragrance of worship to God.

We don't do it to impress people—we do it because we are God's ambassadors. And if Jesus is excellent, then so must we be.

You may not feel like you're there yet. That's okay. Excellence is not a destination—it's a daily decision. Choose to sharpen your gift. Choose to get better. Choose to do your best even when no one's watching.

Remember, excellence is a seed. Keep sowing it, and in due time, the harvest will come.

I believe in you.

Day 7
OBSCURITY IS NOT ALWAYS A CURSE

There are seasons in life when it seems as if everything about you is hidden. No one notices the work you're putting in. No one acknowledges the long nights, the silent tears, or the quiet sacrifices. It feels like you're invisible—doing your best, yet going unnoticed. But hear this clearly: sometimes, **God hides us**. Not to punish us, but to *prepare* us.

God hides you not because you're unworthy, but because you're **not yet fully ready for the weight of visibility.** In His wisdom, He allows a season of obscurity—where you are trained, refined, and strengthened in silence—before the day of your revealing.

In the journey of purpose, obscurity is inevitable. It's not a punishment; it's preparation. It's not rejection; it's refinement. That "backroom" experience is where your character is forged, your integrity is tested, and your roots go deep. What feels like a *hideaway* is really God's divine strategy for your eventual *breakaway*.

So if it seems like no one sees your hard work right now…If no one knows how many midnight hours you've poured into your craft…If no one notices how many times you chose purpose over pleasure…If no one applauds the tears you cried, the prayers you whispered, or the moments you almost gave up but didn't...

Please understand: **it's only a phase.** This will pass. The silence doesn't mean stagnation. It means God is doing something deep in you that the crowd isn't meant to see—not yet.

David wasn't always a king. Long before the throne, there was the field. He was tucked away, caring for sheep, unseen by men—but *seen by God.* And in that hidden season, he was learning to play the harp, to fight wild beasts, and to hear God's voice. The wilderness was shaping him for the palace. The bear and lion were not random attacks—they were divine training for Goliath.

David didn't despise that phase. He stayed faithful, and when the day of public battle came, he didn't shrink. He stood tall. Why? Because he had been preparing when no one was watching.

So don't despise your field. Don't curse your obscurity. It's not your ending; it's your proving ground.

Joseph, too, experienced years of obscurity. Betrayed, enslaved, imprisoned—all while carrying a dream from God.

It must have felt like God had forgotten. But no, Joseph was being refined. He was learning leadership in Potiphar's house. He was learning administration in Pharaoh's prison. And when the moment came to interpret Pharaoh's dream, he was not only ready—he was *elevated*.

The path to purpose will always have a wilderness. Even John the Baptist, the forerunner of Christ, was in the wilderness for years before his voice shook a generation. And when his time came, people *left the cities* to find him. God will bring the right people to you when the preparation is complete.

So don't lose heart. This season is working for you.

Don't give up because your name isn't being called yet. Don't stop because your efforts haven't gone viral. Don't retreat because the applause hasn't come. Heaven sees what man overlooks.

Keep your focus. Keep learning. Keep growing. Keep burning the midnight oil if you must. Keep choosing books over brunch if that's what growth demands. Stay consistent in prayer. Stay anchored in the Word. Keep sharpening your sword. You're not wasting time—you're *investing it*.

David didn't know when Goliath would appear, but he made sure to be ready. He used every fight with the lion and the bear to develop his confidence, his strength, and his testimony. He was building his spiritual résumé.

Don't waste your lion seasons. Don't waste your bear battles. They are not random. They are not pointless. They are dress rehearsals for the giant that will one day launch you into your next level. **Your Goliath is coming, and he must meet you ready.**

It may look like nothing is working right now. You might feel like everything is caving in. But trust me, you are gathering experience. You are storing up wisdom. You are strengthening your spirit. You are being prepared for impact.

The truth is, no one gets to skip the process. Everyone you admire today went through a season like yours. A hidden phase. A waiting room. A quiet climb. They, too, endured moments where quitting felt easier than continuing—but they pressed on. So must you.

Remember, God isn't just interested in what you'll do. He's invested in *who you're becoming.* That's why He takes time to shape you in obscurity. He wants to build a foundation that will last when you're finally seen.

You may not be on the stage yet. You may still be behind the scenes. But you are becoming. You are maturing. You are getting ready.

The **Valley of Elah awaits**. Goliath is on the battlefield. And when your name is called, it will be too late to start training—you must already be equipped.

So keep slaying your lions. Keep writing that book no one is reading yet. Keep praying those prayers no one hears. Keep preparing those sermons no one is inviting you to preach. Keep building that vision that no one else believes in yet.

Because when the moment comes—and it *will*—God will make sure your voice is heard, your light is seen, and your work is rewarded.

And when that day of visibility arrives, it won't be your popularity that sustains you. It will be the strength, wisdom, and humility that were forged in obscurity.

This is not the time to quit.

This is the season to dig deep. To remain faithful. To trust the process.

Because the very gifts you are developing in the secret place are what God will use to announce you in the open place.

Don't be discouraged. Don't rush out of the wilderness. Stay the course. Because soon, the very people who overlooked you will seek you out—not because you made noise, but because you were *prepared*.

You are being hidden now so that you can be revealed in glory later.

Stay faithful.

Stay ready.

Your breakaway is coming.

And I believe in you.

Day 8
MAKE THE MOST OF TIME

Time is one of the most precious gifts God has given to mankind. It is so valuable that even God Himself operates within time when dealing with us on earth. And what's most powerful is that time has been given to everyone in equal measure. Whether you are rich or poor, young or old, educated or uneducated, spiritual or secular, we all receive the same 24 hours in a day. The difference in our outcomes comes down to one thing—how we use it.

The key to life is not necessarily who you know or what you have—it's how you manage your time. In fact, the quality of your life is directly connected to the stewardship of your time. God will give you opportunities, ideas, and even relationships, but if you mismanage your time, you will misuse those blessings.

There are essentially three ways to use time: you can either **waste it**, **spend it**, or **invest it**.

Failures waste time. They are often the ones always "bored," searching for something to fill the silence. They pass hours on end gossiping on the phone, binge-watching endless TV series, or mindlessly scrolling through social media feeds. They spend hours arguing about celebrities or sports, passionately debating which player is better without showing that same passion for their own future. And the truth is, they aren't out of time—they are simply wasting the time they have.

If that describes you, you need to shift your mindset quickly. Time is not just passing—it is *life*. When you waste time, you're wasting life. And unlike money, once time is lost, it cannot be earned back. Ephesians 5:15–16 instructs us to *"walk circumspectly, not as fools but as wise, redeeming the time, because the days are evil."* Redeeming time means making the most of every opportunity. It means being intentional with every hour God gives you.

Then there are those who merely spend time. These are average people. They are not necessarily wasting time, but they are not investing it either. They are simply existing. Their lives are locked in repetitive cycles—wake up, go to work, come home, sleep, and repeat. They don't pursue anything that stretches them. They avoid challenges and resist growth. They have no burning vision, no pressing goals, and no long-term dreams. They have settled into a life of routine. They may be decent people, even responsible—but they are not living *fully*.

God did not create you just to "get by." He didn't breathe His Spirit into you so you could live in survival mode. He called you to thrive, to rule, to subdue, and to walk in dominion (Genesis 1:28). You were made for more than a pay check and a routine. You were made for purpose.

Many people stay stuck in this average cycle because they fear the unknown. They would rather stay in a poorly-paying job than risk stepping out in faith. They avoid investing in themselves because it's uncomfortable. But here's the truth: **you cannot rise beyond your willingness to stretch**. Your next level won't come from comfort; it will come from courage.

Then there are successful people—those who invest their time. These people live with purpose. They wake up each day with a "why" burning in their hearts. They're not driven by entertainment or convenience. They are driven by destiny.

They understand that time is seed. So they plant it into books, into training, into quiet time with God, into meaningful relationships, and into building what God has placed in their hearts. They don't allow every invitation or distraction into their calendar. They have learned the sacred power of "No," because they understand that every "Yes" must serve their assignment.

These people are disciplined. They have dreams and they are not just dreamers—they are doers. They don't just talk about vision; they execute. And even if they're not where they want to be yet, they are moving with purpose. They are progressing. They are growing. They are sowing into their future—and harvest is inevitable.

If this sounds like you, I congratulate you. Because even if the rewards haven't shown up yet, they will. God is faithful to those who steward time well. Galatians 6:9 reminds us, *"And let us not be weary in well doing: for in due season we shall reap, if we faint not."* Every moment invested in your purpose will yield fruit in its time.

What's more, successful people don't hoard success—they share it. They have a heart to lift others as they climb. They understand that true success is not selfish. It's generous. If your elevation doesn't create opportunities for others, it's not success in God's eyes—it's vanity.

These people are not stuck in the rat race. They're not moved by trends or public opinion. They don't live reactively—they live intentionally. They are kings and queens in their domain, not victims of circumstance. They know where they are going, and they surround themselves with others who inspire growth. Proverbs 13:20 says, *"He who walks with the wise grows wise, but a companion of fools suffers harm."* That's why they guard their associations wisely.

So now, the question returns to you. **How are you using your time?** Are you wasting it on things that won't matter in five years? Are you merely spending it in cycles with no growth? Or are you investing it with eternity in view?

You hold the power to decide. There are no shortcuts to success. You must choose—*will I squander or will I invest?* One leads to frustration. The other leads to fruitfulness. Those who invest time become stewards of greatness. Those who waste time eventually look back with regret.

You were not created to be a waster of time. You were called to be a wise investor—building purpose, shaping legacy, and fulfilling destiny with every minute God gives you.

So I challenge you today: put your time to work. Start that book. Enrol in that course. Schedule your prayer retreat. Write that business plan. Serve in your local church. Spend time with your children. Mentor someone. Build what God has put in your hands.

And if you're ready to start investing your time, if you're making the decision to stop squandering and start stewarding—shout it from your heart: *YEAH!*

I believe in you.

Day 9
DOING MORE WITH LESS

There's a saying that goes, "If you chase two rabbits at the same time, both will escape." It's a simple image, but it holds a profound truth about focus. In life, the key to effectiveness is not found in doing more—it's found in doing *less* with greater *intentionality*. Many people think that productivity is about being busy. But the reality is, **busyness is not the same as productivity.**

The truth is, we don't necessarily achieve more by doing more. Sometimes, the path to more is through *less*. Not through laziness or passivity, but through clarity, strategy, and focus. It's the principle of doing more with less—of narrowing your attention to what truly matters and doing that with excellence.

The Bible says in Ecclesiastes 10:10, *"If the ax is dull and one does not sharpen the edge, then he must use more strength; but wisdom brings success."* In other words, wisdom—knowing what to focus on—is what brings results. Not frantic activity. Not exhaustion. Not multitasking. But *focus*.

God created you with specific gifts, strengths, and assignments. Not everything that comes your way is meant for you to do. And not everything you can do is worth doing.

That's why wisdom demands that you evaluate everything that occupies your time and ask yourself: *Is this necessary? Is this fruitful? Is this aligned with my purpose?*

If something is outside your area of strength, consider one of three things: **Delegate, Simplify, or Eliminate.**

Delegate the task to someone who is better suited for it—someone for whom that task is a strength, not a struggle. Delegation is not weakness; it is wisdom. Even Moses, when overwhelmed by the needs of the people, had to be advised by Jethro to appoint leaders and share the load (Exodus 18:17–23). Delegation freed him to focus on what mattered most—hearing from God and leading the people with clarity.

Simplify the task when possible. Not every project requires complexity. Often, we overthink, over-plan, and overcomplicate what could be streamlined with a little wisdom. Simplicity creates clarity. Simplicity frees energy. And simplicity—done right—can multiply your impact.

And then, Eliminate. Yes, some things just don't belong on your list at all. If a task doesn't serve your calling, purpose, or well-being, remove it. Jesus Himself modelled this. He didn't try to be everywhere at once or please everyone. He said in John 5:19, *"The Son can do nothing of Himself, but what He sees the Father do."* That's focus. That's divine alignment. That's clarity of purpose.

One principle that helps drive this home is the **Pareto Principle**, also known as the 80/20 rule. It suggests that 80% of your results often come from 20% of your efforts. Think about that: out of every 10 things you do, only 2 of them likely produce the majority of your success. The other 8 may be consuming energy, time, and attention—but contributing little to no fruit.

This principle changed my life when I embraced it. I started taking inventory of everything I was involved in. I asked, "Which of these truly moves the needle? Which of these aligns with my purpose? Which tasks energize me and bring results?" And the clarity that followed was liberating.

When you begin to live this way, your life becomes lighter, more focused, and more effective. You begin to say *no* more often—not out of rudeness, but out of wisdom. You protect your time like the precious gift it is. You stop being busy and start being *fruitful*.

Even Jesus, the most purposeful Man who ever walked the earth, modelled this. He didn't heal every sick person in Israel. He didn't visit every town. He focused on the people and places the Father sent Him to. And in three years, He fulfilled His mission. Not by being scattered—but by being focused.

Your purpose will not be fulfilled through constant distraction. You cannot master your calling if your energy is divided. A divided mind produces divided outcomes. That's why James 1:8 says, *"A double-minded man is unstable in all his ways."*

Take a moment and do a personal audit. Look at everything on your calendar, your to-do list, and your commitments. Ask yourself honestly: Which of these truly matter? Which align with my God-given assignment? What needs to be delegated, simplified, or eliminated?

Start with clarity. What is your focus for this season? What is your core assignment right now? Every opportunity, request, and demand should be filtered through that focus. If it doesn't serve the mission, it doesn't deserve your energy.

The enemy of greatness is not failure—it's *distraction*. Many people fail not because they lacked talent or opportunity, but because they were spread too thin. They tried to chase too many things. And in the process, they caught nothing.

But if you focus—truly focus—on the few things that matter most, you'll start seeing results that once felt impossible. You'll begin to live in flow, walking in sync with your purpose, your passion, and your assignment.

Let this be your prayer: *"Lord, teach me to number my days, that I may apply my heart unto wisdom."* (Psalm 90:12). In other words, "God, help me manage my time with eternity in view. Help me choose the important over the urgent. Help me do what matters most."

You don't need more hours in a day. You just need to manage your focus. You just need to simplify your priorities. You just need to stop chasing two rabbits and give yourself permission to go after *one* with all your heart.

Don't try to be everywhere, doing everything for everyone. Be where you're called. Do what you're graced to do. Say yes to purpose, and no to distraction.

This is how you live a life of impact. This is how you get results that last. This is how you please God with your time.

And if you're ready to start living focused, intentional, and purpose-driven, then I say to you with joy:

I believe in you.

Day 10
GET TO WORK

So you've bought some books lately, and you've started reading them eagerly. That's wonderful! You've been showing up for webinars, signing up for workshops, attending conferences—your learning journey is in full swing. That's fantastic! You've even found yourself a mentor—someone seasoned and wise—who's been pouring into you, helping you see life, purpose, and potential from a clearer perspective. That's something to be celebrated.

But here's the real question: **What are you doing with all this knowledge?**

Because the truth is, without action, knowledge is nothing more than stored-up potential. It's like collecting seeds and never planting them—no matter how many you have, they'll never produce fruit until they are buried, watered, and nurtured through action. The same is true of everything you're learning.

It's not enough to read. It's not enough to attend. It's not enough to listen. The only thing that transforms your life is what you **do** with what you know.

I've seen people who could quote dozens of authors, recite principles, explain frameworks, and recall entire sermons—

but they remain stuck. Why? Because their heads are full, but their hands are idle. They are always learning, but never applying. Always inspired, but never initiating.

The Bible puts it plainly in James 1:22: *"But be doers of the word, and not hearers only, deceiving yourselves."* That's strong language—deceiving *yourself.* It means you can be deeply convinced you're growing simply because you're learning, but if there is no corresponding action, it's an illusion.

In James 2:17, Scripture takes it even further: *"Thus also faith by itself, if it does not have works, is dead."* Dead faith. Think about that. It's not that the person doesn't believe. It's not that they don't have dreams or even plans. But belief without movement is lifeless. In the Kingdom of God, faith only becomes fruitful when it is partnered with **obedience** and **action**.

So yes, information can change your life—but only **if** it's applied. The books won't transform you until their truths are lived out. The conference won't elevate you unless your decisions change after attending. The mentorship won't propel you unless you start acting on what you've been taught.

In fact, let me tell you something radical: **reading books doesn't change lives.** Only the application of what's inside the book changes lives. Learning is not enough—living what you learn is what matters.

You can't build a life of impact on intentions. No one writes history by merely gathering insight. Greatness is not about what you *know*—it's about what you *do* with what you know. That's why John Mason said, *"Your life story is not written with a pen, but with your actions."*

Let that sink in.

The story people will tell about your life won't be based on how many books lined your shelf, or how many courses you completed. They'll remember what you built, what you gave, what you dared to try, and how you made them feel through your work, your leadership, and your contribution.

Henry Ford put it plainly: *"You can't build a reputation on what you're going to do."* You can talk about it, plan it, dream it, journal about it—but until you take action, it's all smoke and no fire.

Action is the proof of desire. Action is the evidence of faith. Action is the seed that unlocks God's blessing.

Jesus Himself emphasized this in Matthew 7:24–25, saying, *"Therefore everyone who hears these words of Mine and puts them into practice is like a wise man who built his house on the rock."* Wisdom isn't just hearing. It's *doing*. The wise builder isn't the one with the best notes—it's the one who *builds*.

Yes, you will make mistakes when you take action. You may try and fail. You might not get it right the first time. But even failure teaches more than inaction ever will. When you act, you gain experience. You grow in discernment. You stretch your faith. You become someone who's not just full of knowledge—but someone who's fruitful in life.

So today, I challenge you to move beyond inspiration and toward implementation.

What did that book tell you to do? Do it.

What did that sermon stir in your heart? Act on it.

What did your mentor urge you to consider? Take the first step.

Don't wait for the perfect moment. Don't wait until you feel "ready." Start with what you have, where you are, and take one step. God blesses *movement*. God responds to faith in motion. Remember the lepers in Luke 17:14? Jesus told them, *"Go, show yourselves to the priests,"* and it was **as they went** that they were healed. Their healing came *in motion*.

That's how God works. He partners with the **doers**. Not the perfect. Not the polished. But the willing. The ones who say, "Lord, I may not have it all figured out, but I'll obey what I know."

There's no shortcut around it. No matter how much you know, how many notes you take, or how inspired you feel—without action, nothing changes.

So let today be the day you move. Let today be the day you stop sitting on potential and start building purpose. Let this be the day you silence procrastination with discipline and drown fear with bold steps of faith.

God has already given you the knowledge, the grace, and the capacity. Now He's waiting on your obedience.

Get to work.

And as you do—I believe in you.

Day 11
BENEFITS OF CONSISTENCY!

Consistency is the quiet but powerful force behind all lasting success. It may not always be glamorous, but it is always effective. Hard work without consistency is like owning a luxury car without an engine—it looks good on the outside but has no power to move forward. Consistency is what fuels progress. Without it, you'll keep starting over again and again, never building momentum, never gaining ground.

If you truly desire to go far in life and fulfil the purpose God has placed in your heart, consistency cannot be negotiable. Everyone on this earth, at some point, has battled the voice of inconsistency. It often creeps in when the excitement wears off, when results are slow, or when challenges arise. Many begin a journey strong, only to let go too soon because they don't see immediate rewards. But lasting success is reserved for those who stay on the path—even when it's uphill.

If you are going to reach the promised land God has revealed to you, you must be consistently on the journey. The road may be long and narrow, but it leads somewhere glorious. Let me share with you ten powerful benefits of staying consistent:

1. Consistency communicates your value.

When you keep showing up—especially when it's hard—you communicate seriousness and reliability. People begin to take you seriously. Your value increases in the eyes of others because they know you're not just chasing trends, but you're committed to something meaningful. Consistency says, "I'm not here for applause—I'm here for purpose." People respect those who stay the course. Successful people aren't merely talented—they are those who kept showing up long after others quit.

2. Consistency helps you get better.

You won't be great at something overnight. Mastery comes through repetition. The more you do a thing, the more you learn, adjust, and improve. Mistakes don't disqualify you—they educate you. Consistency gives you room to fail, learn, and grow stronger. Over time, you become skilled, refined, and excellent—not because you were perfect from the start, but because you didn't give up.

3. Consistency gives you clarity and expands your horizon.

The more consistent you are in your pursuit, the clearer your purpose becomes. Doubt fades, focus sharpens, and vision expands. You stop second-guessing and start walking with confidence. Consistency builds rhythm, and that rhythm creates mental space for creativity, innovation, and deeper thinking. If you stay committed, what once felt impossible will soon feel natural.

4. Consistency attracts valuable relationships.

People are drawn to those who are consistent. When others see that you're serious and dependable, they want to join you. Vision requires consistency to grow. No one wants to run with a leader who quits halfway. As you stay consistent, God will send destiny helpers—those who will catch your vision, support your purpose, and walk alongside you to see it fulfilled.

5. Consistency increases your self-confidence.

Confidence isn't something you're born with—it's something you build. Every time you follow through on your commitment, you tell your mind, "I can be trusted." That internal trust becomes confidence. You don't gain self-respect by being perfect; you gain it by being faithful. Consistency strengthens your belief in yourself and in the God who called you.

6. Consistency gets you noticed.

Whether you're building a business, a ministry, or a personal brand—visibility matters. And nothing boosts visibility like consistency. When you keep showing up, people eventually notice. Even if no one pays attention at first, stay the course. The world takes notice of those who persevere. Proverbs 22:29 says, *"Do you see a man skilled in his work? He will stand before kings."* Skill comes through consistency—and skill opens doors.

7. Consistency motivates you.

Some days, motivation will be nowhere to be found. But when you commit to consistency, it creates its own momentum. The simple act of showing up daily can reignite your passion. Even when the fire feels low, consistency stirs the coals. Over time, your habits begin to pull you forward, even when your feelings don't.

8. Consistency gives you momentum.

Momentum is that forward push that builds over time. Every small, consistent step contributes to your overall progress. It may not seem like much in the moment, but step by step, you are moving forward. And once momentum kicks in, you gain speed. You begin to see results. Progress breeds more progress. It's like pushing a heavy wheel—hard at first, but once it starts rolling, it becomes unstoppable.

9. Consistency creates impact.

Your influence grows when you stay the course. People may not notice you at first. They may overlook your efforts. But if you keep showing up, keep serving, keep giving, your work will start to touch lives. Impact isn't made in one grand moment—it's made through steady deposits of service, love, and excellence. And one day, those deposits become legacy.

10. Consistency creates a perception of quality.

People equate consistency with excellence. When you continue delivering value over time, you become known for it. You build a name, a reputation, a brand. You become the go-to person in your area of assignment. People trust what they see consistently. If you want to be known as a principality in your field, then you must consistently show up with excellence.

So, do you now see why you cannot afford to be inconsistent in your journey?

Your purpose, your calling, your destiny—none of it will manifest without the fuel of consistency. No matter how anointed you are, how gifted or passionate you may be, **if you are not consistent, your potential will never become reality.**

God has placed something in your hands. Don't treat it casually. There is room for you to grow. There is space for your influence to spread. But your consistency must speak louder than your excuses.

Stay faithful. Stay diligent. Keep showing up.

Because I promise you—if you commit to six months of focused, prayerful consistency, your life will not remain the same.

And I believe in you.

Day 12
POWER OF ACCESS TO THE RIGHT PEOPLE

There's something dangerous about familiarity—it blinds us to the value that surrounds us. You might be walking daily with someone anointed, gifted, or graced, and still miss out on the transformation they carry simply because you've allowed your eyes to grow dim with over-familiarity.

You have access to a person of value—and you're taking it for granted. There are people around you doing exceptionally well, yet you've minimized their worth. Potential mentors, coaches, and destiny helpers are within reach, but because they're familiar—friends, colleagues, acquaintances—you've overlooked the very vessel God may have placed in your life to lift you.

This is no small matter. In the divine economy, honour is the currency that grants access to grace. Throughout Scripture, miracles often flowed when people recognized and honoured the vessels God had positioned in their lives. And conversely, many missed out—or were even judged—because they disrespected those vessels.

Take the woman with the issue of blood. She had been sick for 12 years, suffering in silence, outcast and weary. But when Jesus passed by, she didn't say, "He's just another preacher." She didn't hesitate. She understood the urgency and uniqueness of the moment. Her heart told her, "This might be the only chance you get." And with determination, she reached out and touched the hem of His garment. That simple act of faith, anchored in honour, changed her story forever.

"For she said to herself, 'If only I may touch His garment, I shall be made well.'" (Matthew 9:21) She didn't need a conversation. She didn't need a miracle appointment. All she needed was a point of contact with grace.

Now imagine if she had taken Jesus for granted—another teacher, another face in the crowd. Her miracle would have walked right past her. That's what over-familiarity does—it closes the eyes of discernment and keeps people stuck when they were meant to rise.

In Luke 10, we read of Jesus visiting the home of Mary and Martha. One chose to sit and glean; the other chose to serve. Both had good intentions, but only one discerned the divine moment correctly. Jesus said of Mary, *"She has chosen that good part, and it will not be taken away from her."* (Luke 10:42) Mary knew the weight of the moment. She refused to let the demands of culture, expectation, or responsibility rob her of access to divine wisdom.

Contrast this with Bartimaeus, the blind beggar in Mark 10. He couldn't see Jesus, but he could hear that grace was passing by. And he shouted! Loudly. Repeatedly. He wasn't going to let the fear of people, embarrassment, or pride stop him. His persistence, rooted in honour, got Jesus' attention. *"What do you want Me to do for you?"* Jesus asked. *"That I may receive my sight,"* he answered. And he did. Because he recognized the moment—and seized it.

Now, consider the other side of this truth. In 2 Kings 2, Elisha—the prophet of God—is mocked by some youths for his appearance. They call him "baldhead". But what seemed like a joke carried a fatal consequence. *"He turned around, pronounced a curse in the name of the Lord, and two bears came out of the woods and mauled forty-two of the youths."* (2 Kings 2:24)

What was their sin? Disregard. Dishonour. They failed to discern the value of the man in front of them. It cost them their lives.

This principle still holds today. When you trivialize the people God has placed in your life, you forfeit the blessings tied to them. The wisdom they carry, the insight they possess, the favour on their lives—it becomes inaccessible to you when you treat them as common.

Don't make that mistake.

Many of the people who can shape your future, open doors, challenge your thinking, or correct your path are not loud or flashy. They may not even have material wealth. But they carry something divine. Something weighty. Their words are gold. Their scars are proof. Their journey is a textbook of experience and grace.

You may think you don't need anyone—but God never designed us to be islands. He brings people to usher us into seasons. He uses people to bless, instruct, sharpen, and correct us. Don't reject the very people He has assigned to your destiny.

When you meet such people, don't start with asking for money or favours. Don't look at their shoes or their car. Instead, open your heart to the grace on their lives. Offer them value. Ask questions. Serve where you can. Sometimes, the greatest access comes not from asking for help, but from offering service.

Some of the greatest mentors will never advertise themselves. You must discern them. You must honour them. You must pursue wisdom with humility.

That old man who doesn't know how to use social media may carry a grace that could unlock your next level. That quiet woman who isn't very eloquent may have walked with God long enough to speak one sentence that could change your life. Don't despise the gift because of the wrapping.

Even when people offer you free resources, teachings, or opportunities—take them seriously. Free doesn't mean worthless. Sometimes the most valuable treasures come disguised as ordinary things.

So here's what you need to do:

Make contact.

Be intentional.

Don't wait for a stage to connect—start with a conversation.

Ask questions.

Listen deeply.

Be humble.

Be patient.

Offer value.

Serve sincerely.

Learn diligently.

Don't expect miracles on your terms—just stay close, and miracles will find you.

Some of the greatest breakthroughs in life are not a result of striving but of honour. Miracles happen when you honour people of value. And many delays in destiny happen when you dishonour those God has sent.

You don't need to meet everyone. Just honour the ones God has placed around you.

And as you honour grace, grace will lift you.

I believe in you.

Day 13
LIVE FOR SOMETHING!

It is not enough to have lived. We should be determined to live for something

Winston S. Churchill

It is not enough to merely exist, you must live for something. You must live life with intentionality. Winston Churchill once said, "It is not enough to have lived. We should be determined to live for something." And indeed, nothing is more tragic than going through life without ever discovering or fulfilling the purpose for which you were born.

You see, the most painful thing is not death itself—it's dying without ever having truly lived. It's reaching the end of your days only to look back and realise you've drifted through life like a leaf in the wind, never anchored, never purposed, never intentional. And for many, this realisation comes too late—when their time is gone, and nothing can be recovered.

Imagine standing before God at the end of your life, not as someone who rebelled, but as someone who was saved yet wasted the life that was meant to glorify Him. Yes, you may be born again, your name written in the Lamb's Book of Life, but your impact on earth was minimal because you never lived with purpose. Salvation is the beginning of the journey, not the end. It opens the door to eternal life, but also to a life of assignment, impact, and responsibility on this side of eternity.

There is a scripture that shook me to my core and transformed my understanding of salvation:

"I said in my heart, 'God shall judge the righteous and the wicked, For there is a time for every purpose and for every work.'"— Ecclesiastes 3:17 (NKJV)

Did you catch that? God will judge not only the wicked but also the righteous. And what will be the measure of that judgement? Purpose and work. What you did with your life. Not just that you were saved, but whether you fulfilled your assignment. Whether you lived for something greater than yourself.

We are not saved merely to escape hell. We are saved to reveal God's glory—to reflect His nature and accomplish His will on the earth. We are saved to be light in the darkness, salt in a tasteless world, vessels through which heaven touches earth. But this can only happen when we start living for something bigger than ourselves.

Too many believers are caught up in the illusion that being born again is the full expression of their Christian life. But truthfully, it is only the beginning. When you came to Christ, He didn't just save your soul; He called you into purpose. He marked you for impact. He planted something within you that must be expressed, something that the world needs.

To live for something is to live for purpose. Purpose is the reason for your existence—it is the divine intention behind your design. You were not randomly created. You were born with gifts, passions, burdens, and callings that are meant to be aligned with a divine assignment. And until you begin to live in that assignment, you may be breathing, but you are not truly living.

Living for something means refusing to waste your life on trivial pursuits. It means refusing to be swayed by the pressures of culture or the mediocrity of the crowd. It means refusing to drift, and choosing instead to live with focus, with meaning, and with fire.

Unfortunately, many people are living accidental lives. They wake up, go to work, pay bills, scroll through social media, go to sleep—and repeat. Day after day. Year after year. With no sense of divine mission. No clarity of purpose. No legacy in view. Friend, that is not living. That is existing.

You must not let your life be defined by survival. Your purpose is not just to "get by." It is to make a difference. It is to glorify God with your gifts. It is to leave the world better than you met it. Purposeful living begins with asking yourself: "What has God called me to do in this season?" and "Am I walking in alignment with His divine assignment for my life?"

Purpose is not always about something dramatic or public. It may not be a pulpit or a stage. It could be raising godly children, mentoring the next generation, writing books that inspire transformation, building businesses that fund the Gospel, or serving in obscurity with excellence and faithfulness. The key is obedience. Fulfilment doesn't come from prominence—it comes from alignment.

When you live for purpose:

- You wake up with direction.
- You endure hardship with hope.
- You say "no" to distractions with conviction.
- You overcome temptations because your eyes are fixed on the goal.

- You live intentionally, knowing your time is a resource, your gifts are tools, and your life is a message.

The truth is, you will give an account—not only for your salvation but for your stewardship. What did you do with what God gave you? What did you build with the life He entrusted to you? What impact did you make in your family, your generation, your sphere of influence?

One day, your life will flash before your eyes. Will it be worth watching? Will it reflect obedience, sacrifice, and purpose? Or will it be filled with regret for roads not taken and assignments left unfulfilled?

Hear this: you were born to live for something. God did not create you to blend in. He created you to stand out. He fashioned you for good works that He prepared in advance (Ephesians 2:10). You carry a unique blend of experiences, talents, and graces that no one else has. The world is waiting for what you carry.

Don't waste your life. Don't drift. Don't bury your purpose beneath fear, comfort, or laziness. Rise up and live with intention. Live with urgency. Live for God and for His purpose.

Whether you are young or old, educated or not, just starting out or in a new season, the call to purpose is still valid. If you are breathing, God still has work for you to do.

You had better be living your life on purpose—and for purpose.

I believe in you.

Day 14
THE VOICES IN YOUR LIFE

Be careful if all the people around you do is applaud you.

We live in a time where everyone craves validation and affirmation. We surround ourselves with people who sing our praises and echo our opinions, calling it "positivity." But if your circle only affirms you and never corrects you—if they only say what you want to hear and never what you *need* to hear—then, dear friend, you are walking on dangerous ground.

We must never mistake applause for accountability. One fuels your ego; the other saves your destiny.

The need for truth-tellers in your life cannot be overstated. These are the people who love you enough to risk offending you. They are not impressed by your charisma, accomplishments, or influence. They are not drawn in by the hype. They see beyond your performance and speak to the person. They are your lifeline.

My father in the Lord, Pastor David Adelowo, once said something profound: *"The devil thrives in isolation."* When you disconnect yourself from people who carry the truth—people who challenge, correct, and sharpen you—you give room for deception to grow. You begin to believe you are right in your own eyes. You become vulnerable to error, pride, and destruction.

"Where there is no counsel, the people fall; But in the multitude of counsellors there is safety."— Proverbs 11:14 (NKJV)

God never designed us to grow in isolation. That's why He places us in families, in churches, in communities. He surrounds us with spiritual leaders, mentors, pastors, and friends—not just for comfort, but for *correction*. Even Jesus, the Son of God, surrounded Himself with people. He engaged in conversations, accepted feedback, and remained accountable to the Father. If He didn't isolate Himself, why should we?

Yet many in this generation have glorified the idea of being "independent." We love our space. We block people at the slightest rebuke. We walk away from tough conversations. We ghost those who confront us. We prefer "vibes only" relationships—feel-good companionships that never stretch us.

But hear me: growth doesn't happen in comfort. It happens when we are challenged. It happens when someone points out the broccoli in your teeth, so to speak—when someone says, "You're better than this," "That decision is unwise," or "You're slipping spiritually." You don't grow from praise. You grow from pruning.

Lions, when hunting, never attack the group. They wait for one sheep or antelope to stray from the herd. Once it isolates itself, it becomes vulnerable. That's exactly how the devil works. He targets those who walk alone, those who sever ties with people of wisdom, those who cut off the voices that challenge them. He whispers, "They don't like you. They're too hard on you. You don't need them." But the real agenda is to weaken you, distract you, and destroy you.

"Faithful are the wounds of a friend, But the kisses of an enemy are deceitful."— Proverbs 27:6 (NKJV)

True friends, true mentors, true leaders will sometimes *wound* you. Not because they hate you, but because they love you too deeply to watch you self-destruct. Their correction may sting, but it will save you. Their words may pierce, but they will preserve you. On the contrary, flattery from those who are afraid to offend you can slowly ruin you.

Let me ask you this: who have you pushed away because they told you the truth?

Who did you call "toxic" simply because they corrected you? Who did you label "negative" or "controlling" because they wouldn't let you drift? Who did you walk away from because they challenged you to grow?

Perhaps it's time to reconsider. Not everyone who upset you was wrong. Not everyone who rebuked you was against you. Some of them were divinely placed in your life to keep you from falling. Some were lifelines disguised as obstacles.

We need to do better.

In fact, each of us needs at least two or three people in our lives who can boldly call us out when we're going astray. People who are not afraid of your status, your title, or your achievements. People who care more about your soul than your feelings. These are your real allies.

Let me give you three simple checkpoints. Ask yourself:

1. **Do they genuinely love me and want the best for me?**

   If yes, their correction comes from a place of concern, not criticism. They aren't just trying to pull you down—they are trying to pull you up.

2. **Do they consistently tell me the truth, no matter what?**

   These are people who speak up even when it's uncomfortable, even when you don't want to hear it, even when everyone else is silent.

3. **Are they still learning how to correct me without hurting me**

   They may not always get the tone or timing right, but their intention is right. They are not perfect—but they are protective. Don't discard the message because the delivery wasn't flawless.

If you answered "yes" to those questions, then friend, you need those voices back in your life. Apologise if you need to. Reconnect if necessary. Humble yourself and rebuild those bridges. Because your success, safety, and spiritual growth may depend on it.

Don't be the person who silences every critic and embraces every flatterer. That's a recipe for destruction. Instead, cultivate a circle of voices—diverse, bold, honest, loving—who will call out the gold in you, confront the flaws in you, and cheer for the greatness in you.

A balanced life isn't built on validation alone. It's built on a blend of encouragement and accountability. Praise lifts your spirit, but correction shapes your soul.

You were never meant to do life alone. God puts people in our lives as mirrors, guides, and guardians. Cherish them. Honour them. Learn from them. Because in the multitude of wise counsel, there is safety, strength, and success.

I believe in you.

Day 15
YOU ARE NOT YOUR BODY

You are not your body.

You are your spirit.

Let that truth sink in. You are not just flesh and bone. You are not simply a biological machine or a random product of evolution. You are not an advanced animal with superior reasoning. No—you are spirit. Created in the image and likeness of God.

"Then God said, 'Let Us make man in Our image, according to Our likeness...'"— *Genesis 1:26a*

This verse isn't poetic fluff. It is your origin story. You came from God. He made you like Himself. He is Spirit, and so are you. The real "you" is not your hairstyle, your body size, your accent, or your fingerprint. The real you is your spirit man.

And that real you—your spirit—is eternal. While your body grows old, tires, wrinkles, and eventually returns to dust, your spirit will live forever. That alone should change how you prioritize your life.

But here's the tension: though your spirit is who you really are, you're housed in a body, and your soul—your mind, will, and emotions—sits in the middle like a battleground. There is a constant tug-of-war. Your spirit wants to do what is pleasing to God. Your flesh wants what pleases itself. Your soul is the referee. And guess what? Whoever gets fed the most will win.

Joyce Meyer captured this struggle so well in her book, *Battlefield of the Mind*. Your mind is ground zero. Every temptation, every doubt, every desire, every insecurity—it all starts in your thoughts. That's why it is so crucial to renew your mind daily, feeding it with the Word of God, the voice of the Spirit, and truth that strengthens your inner man.

"For those who are led by the Spirit of God are the children of God." — *Romans 8:14*

The question is: who is leading you? Is it your flesh, or your spirit? Are you investing in the man within, or are you so consumed with your body that you've forgotten what really matters?

We live in a generation that glorifies the outer shell. We spend money on skincare, fashion, food, and gadgets. And while there's nothing wrong with taking care of your body, it is foolish to spend more on the container than you do on the content.

Your body is a house. Your spirit is the occupant. Yet, many people repaint the house, decorate the porch, and ignore the one who lives inside.

What if you flipped the script?

What if you spent more time, more money, more energy on developing your spirit man?

What if your next budget included spiritual books, audio sermons, devotionals, retreats, prayer nights, fasting days, study time, and soul-refining fellowship?

What if your soul's well-being mattered to you more than your next gym session?

The truth is, those who grow spiritually do so intentionally. They feed their spirit like it's their first responsibility—because it is. They understand that peace, purpose, clarity, and strength are not found in trendy lifestyles or physical indulgences, but in deep spiritual alignment with God.

"And do not be conformed to this world, but be transformed by the renewing of your mind…" — *Romans 12:2a*

Transformation doesn't come through wishful thinking. It comes through the renewing of your mind—which is another way of saying, *feeding your spirit through the soul.* As you meditate on the Word, worship, seek truth, and yield to the Holy Spirit, you allow your spirit to rise above the cravings of the flesh.

It's like tending a fire. If you keep adding wood, it burns bright. If you ignore it, it dies out. The same is true with your spirit. The more you nurture it, the more it dominates the flesh.

Think about this: when your spirit is strong, you are not easily offended. You discern better. You make wiser choices. You resist sin more effectively. You're not tossed around by every emotional storm or cultural trend. You carry peace. You radiate purpose. You overflow with power.

But when your spirit is weak—when it is starved—you become irritable, confused, indecisive, carnal, and fearful. Why? Because your body and soul have taken over, while the spirit man sits starved and silent.

You cannot live a purposeful life disconnected from your spirit.

You cannot walk in dominion when your inner man is feeble. You cannot fulfil destiny with a strong body and a malnourished spirit.

That is why you must invest. Start today.

Invest in prayer.

Invest in worship.

Invest in Scripture.

Invest in silence and solitude with God.

Invest in godly books, courses, mentors, teachings, and community.

It's not about religion or rules. It's about alignment. It's about reality. Your purpose cannot find full expression until your spirit takes the lead.

Let me put it this way: When your spirit is aligned with God, your mind becomes clearer, your emotions settle, and your body follows suit. That's when you begin to walk in full capacity—spirit, soul, and body, as God designed.

"Though outwardly we are wasting away, yet inwardly we are being renewed day by day." — *2 Corinthians 4:16*

The body shrinks with age. The spirit grows stronger when fed. So ask yourself: which part of you are you feeding more?

If you want to live a life of impact and fulfilment, then start by feeding the part of you that will outlast time. You'll soon see your potential awaken. Your purpose will spark to life. You'll feel power surging through your convictions. And your decisions will carry eternal weight.

The real you is waiting to rise. Let him rise.

I believe in you.

Day 16
HOW TO BEGIN TO ENJOY PRAYER

I was having a conversation with one of my best friends just some time ago. We had just finished a meeting and decided to catch up. One hour turned into almost two, and before we knew it, we had drifted from one topic to another—life transitions, growth, faith, lessons we were learning. It was rich, fluid, unplanned, yet deeply nourishing. Eventually, we had to call it a day with promises to pick up the conversation again when next we speak.

That's what friendship looks like: unforced, natural, honest.

And it made me think—what if our prayer life looked like that? What if communion with God was as genuine and free-flowing as a heart-to-heart with your best friend? What if prayer stopped being a task on your Christian to-do list and started becoming the joy of your day?

You see, one of the primary reasons many believers struggle with prayer is because they approach it like a chore - from a place of duty, not relationship. It's not always effective when prayer becomes a religious obligation; something we're *supposed* to do. Like a morning chore, a checklist item before breakfast. And so, we offer it to God like a burnt offering, not realising that what God desires more than our words is our presence.

Prayer was never meant to be a cold, repetitive ritual. It is meant to be *communion*. It is fellowship. It is intimacy. It is relational exchange between Father and child, Creator and creation, friend and friend.

"No longer do I call you servants... but I have called you friends." — *John 15:15*

Jesus desires friendship, not formality. But many of us are praying with form but without connection. We throw words toward heaven, but we don't stay long enough to listen. We pray like we're performing, not conversing.

Let me ask you—do you ever feel like prayer is just one-sided?

Imagine you call your friend every day. You say "hello," then spend 10 minutes talking, venting, asking, rambling... and just when your friend is about to respond, you hang up. Not once, but every time. What kind of relationship would that be?

That's what many of us are doing to the Holy Spirit. We speak—but we don't listen. We call—but we don't wait for a response. We pour out—but we don't pause to receive.

That's not communion. That's a monologue.

And no real friendship can thrive on monologues.

True prayer is a dialogue. You talk to God, and He talks back to you. You share your heart, and He shares His. You speak, and then you *wait*.

"My sheep hear My voice, and I know them, and they follow Me." — *John 10:27*

Yes, you can hear God. Not just preachers and prophets. Not just special people. You, as a child of God, can be led by His voice. But His voice is clearest when your heart is still. When your mind is quiet. When you stop rushing out of His presence the moment you've finished your part of the conversation.

What would happen if, after every time you prayed, you sat still for another five… ten… fifteen minutes? What if you leaned in with faith that the Holy Spirit is present, seated right across from you, ready to respond?

Because He is. The Holy Spirit is not distant or abstract. He is your Companion, your Comforter, your Counsellor. He is always speaking—you just need to posture your heart to listen.

"Be still, and know that I am God…" — *Psalm 46:10*

In that stillness, you begin to sense Him—nudging your thoughts, illuminating scripture, stirring your spirit. As you write down what you're receiving, you begin to recognise the sound of His voice. Over time, you cultivate a rhythm with God—a beautiful, ongoing conversation that never really ends.

Some of the most life-changing moments happen not during prayer, but *after* prayer—in those sacred moments when you linger in His presence and hear Him speak.

He might whisper to you about your future.

He might correct a wrong motive.

He might unveil your next step.

He might give you wisdom for your marriage, your business, your community.

He might even give you insight into your generation, or reveal what's coming in the next decade.

But you'll miss all of that if you treat prayer like a speech and not a friendship.

Prayer is not about fancy words. It's not about length. It's not about posture. It's about the **heart**. It's about desiring to know God and be known by Him.

Let me remind you—Jesus didn't die just to save you from sin. He died to reconcile you back to a **relationship** with the Father. And in that relationship, conversation is key.

"Call to Me, and I will answer you, and show you great and mighty things, which you do not know." — *Jeremiah 33:3*

That's an open invitation. God is not silent. He desires to speak to you more than you desire to hear Him.

So let me challenge you today:

Don't just pray. **Fellowship.**

Don't just speak. **Listen.**

Don't just check in. **Dwell.**

Prayer should feel like talking to your closest friend. It should be honest, simple, and daily. Sometimes it's intense.

Sometimes it's light-hearted. Sometimes it's emotional. Sometimes it's quiet. But always—it's a conversation.

Take time to pray.

Take time to listen.

Take time to **be** with Him.

You will be surprised how much God wants to talk to you—if only you will make room for Him.

He's waiting.

Can you hear Him?

I believe in you.

Day 17
YOU ARE THE LIGHT OF THE WORLD!

Not too long ago, I walked into my kids' room and something felt off—it wasn't as bright as it used to be. At first, I didn't immediately catch what had changed. Then I looked up—and there it was. One of the two light bulbs had burned out.

The room was still lit, but the difference was obvious. The brightness wasn't the same. One bulb was doing its best, but the absence of the other was deeply felt.

As I reflected on this scene, the Holy Spirit began to whisper truths to my heart. What seemed like a minor observation became a powerful revelation. I'd love to share with you nine important lessons this moment taught me:

1. You are the light of the world, and you are made to shine.

Don't dim your light for anyone or anything. You were not saved to hide—you were saved to shine. God placed His glory in you so you could radiate it in a dark world. The devil is the only one who belongs in darkness; as a child of God, your identity is anchored in light.

"You are the light of the world. A city that is set on a hill cannot be hidden."— *Matthew 5:14*

Let this truth settle in your heart: You are meant to be seen for the glory of God.

2. To not shine is to forfeit your essence.

Light that refuses to shine has already lost its identity. To believe that you have nothing to offer is to believe a lie from the pit of hell. You have everything it takes to be a blessing. You were born loaded, gifted, and sent here for a purpose. Your light is your contribution—don't bury it.

3. Your significance is in your shine.

A bulb without light is no different from a rock on the floor. Potential only matters when it's activated. A light that doesn't shine is no better than a light that's never been installed. Let your impact be felt. Let your significance be known. Shine where God has placed you, and do it boldly.

4.If all God's children shine, the world will be full of His glory.

Right now, darkness is having a field day—on social media, in culture, in conversations. But the truth is, darkness only thrives where light stays silent. God's children must rise and shine in every space—online and offline. Whether it's with your voice, your gifts, your creativity, or your kindness—let the light of Christ flow through you.

"For the earnest expectation of the creation eagerly waits for the revealing of the sons of God."— *Romans 8:19*

5. We need each other to brighten the world.

Don't dim someone else's light just because you're still figuring out how to turn yours on. Celebrate the brightness of others. Let their light inspire yours. The sky is big enough for every star. God made room for all of us to shine. Instead of competing, let's complement one another. There's more than enough room at the top for everyone who's called.

6. If you don't shine, you might be replaced.

It's a sobering truth. God's agenda will move forward—with or without us. If you're unwilling to shine, He'll raise someone else who will. Don't be the one who has to be replaced. The world needs what you carry. Your gift is needed. Your voice is valuable. Your light matters.

"Every tree that does not bear good fruit is cut down and thrown into the fire."— *Matthew 7:19*

7. Many destinies are tied to your shine.

There are people whose lives will only change when *you* shine. Your obedience becomes their breakthrough. Your visibility becomes their inspiration. Your courage becomes their deliverance. So please, for their sake, light up your corner of the world. Someone's healing, purpose, or calling may depend on it.

8. If you don't shine, you'll remain invisible.

Branding, influence, impact—they all begin with visibility. But if you choose to hide, you rob the world of the message God placed in you. It's time to stop apologising for who you are. Your story, your voice, your journey—these are the very things that will draw people to Christ through you.

9. When you shine, you're too hot to handle.

Light doesn't just illuminate—it burns. It refines. It repels darkness. When you walk in the fullness of your calling, you become a threat to the enemy. He'll try to dim your light, discourage your heart, and distract your purpose. But don't give him a foothold. Burn with passion. Blaze with purpose. Be bold and unstoppable.

"Arise, shine; for your light has come! And the glory of the Lord is risen upon you."— *Isaiah 60:1*

Dear friend, don't settle for a half-lit life. Don't live beneath the brightness God designed you to carry. Whether you're a bulb in the corner of a child's room or a blazing torch in a stadium, you were made to shine.

Light up the space you've been planted in. Illuminate your generation.

Carry the fire of God boldly.

I believe in you.

Day 18
THERE IS MORE TO YOU

My batteries died.

That morning, my wireless mouse stopped working completely. A few days earlier, my computer had flashed a warning—"Low battery, replace soon." But I ignored it. I pushed it off.

Now, here I was. Stuck.

So I finally replaced the batteries. As I was about to toss the old ones into the bin, something stopped me. "Wait a minute," I thought, "these batteries might still work in something else."

So I popped them into one of our wall clocks.

To my surprise, the clock sprang to life. As though I'd inserted brand-new batteries.

That moment hit me deeply. I stood there holding the empty mouse and staring at the ticking clock, and the Holy Spirit began to speak. It was as though God whispered, "This is you. This is how I see my children."

You may have felt like you've failed. Maybe you've been told your best days are behind you. Maybe heartbreak has made you numb. Rejection has crushed you. Your environment has convinced you that your worth is gone. That you're drained. Used up. Done for.

But listen to me: *you are not done.*

The fact that one system didn't recognize your worth anymore doesn't mean you've lost your value. Just like those batteries, your life might have stopped "working" in one area, but there is still power left in you. There's still a purpose. There's still a use. You are *not* disposable.

God doesn't discard people. He redeems them. He repositions them.

Maybe you've been through:

- Heartbreak
- Pain
- Failure
- Abuse
- Discouragement
- Rejection
- Depression
- A tough upbringing

But those things are not the sum total of who you are. They may be *part* of your story, but they are not *the end* of it.

There is still more to you.

Even if people have written you off, God hasn't. Even if you've sidelined yourself, God is still calling your name. He has not changed His mind about your purpose. You are not forgotten.

Remember what happened at the wedding in Cana? The wine ran out. It seemed like the joy and celebration were over. But Jesus stepped in and gave them the best wine at the very end. That's what He does—He saves the best for last.

"You have kept the good wine until now!"
— John 2:10

God still has an assignment for you. He still has a platform for you. He still has impact waiting on the other side of your obedience. Your past is no match for His plans. Your scars are not too deep for His power.

And yes, you still carry gifts. You still carry purpose. You still carry glory.

Think about David. A shepherd boy—overlooked, forgotten, tending sheep in the wilderness. Yet his wilderness did not disqualify him from the palace. In fact, it *prepared* him for it. The same slingshot he used in private became his ticket to national recognition.

There is a palace ahead of you.

But you can't give up now.

You can't throw in the towel.

You can't disappear.

You can't surrender to despair.

You are still useful.

You are still needed.

You still carry power.

You carry grace.

You carry divine potential.

Even if life has used you, reduced you, misunderstood you, or mishandled you—God still knows how to bring purpose out of your pain.

So hold on. Don't stop now. There's something the world still needs from you. Something *only you* can bring. You might feel drained, but the Spirit of God still flows through you. If you'll let Him reposition you—just like those batteries—He'll show you exactly where your strength is still needed.

There's still more.

More to become.

More to offer.

More to build.

More to release.

Let your story rise again. Your next chapter might just be your best.

I believe in you.

Day 19
QUIT TALKING, START WORKING

No one is impressed by your dream.

Why?

Because dreams are common. Everyone has one. From the child in kindergarten to the corporate executive, from the broke visionary on the street to the billionaire entrepreneur—everyone's got a dream. So what makes yours different?

That's why shouting "I have a dream!" isn't enough.

When Martin Luther King Jr. uttered those iconic words, it wasn't the statement that made history—it was the *sacrifice*, the *action*, the *relentless pursuit of change* that followed those words. He wasn't asleep. He didn't rest in the comfort of a dream. He *moved*.

Sadly, many people prefer to stay in the dream because reality is often brutal. Dreams are comfortable, but real change is costly. And while dreaming feels safe, dreaming alone changes nothing. Dreams won't move the world—you will. Through *action*.

"Faith by itself, if it does not have works, is dead."
— James 2:17

In the same way, dreams without action are lifeless—empty visions without the breath of courage and obedience. It's not enough to dream. It's not even enough to believe in the dream. What gives your dream credibility is movement. What gives it a voice is execution.

You don't win a football game by dreaming of goals—you win by *scoring* them. Running. Shooting. Persisting. A dream without pursuit is fantasy. A dream with action becomes a testimony.

Too often, we hear people say, "I'm just waiting on God." But truthfully? God is waiting on you. He placed the dream in your heart to *ignite* your movement, not to *excuse* your stagnation. A dream that God gives you is an invitation to partner with Him in birthing something divine.

But you've got to push.

You've got to *labour* in the vision.

You can't expect the dream to work if you won't work on the dream.

Talk is cheap. Execution is costly.

Don't just talk about it—*build* it. Start small if you must, but start!

- Make the call.
- Send the email.
- Enquire about the training.
- Write the outline.
- Draft the plan.
- Record the video.
- Knock on that door.
- Apply for that grant.
- Register that business.

Do something about the dream today. Let your steps speak louder than your status. Every action you take becomes a brick in the foundation of your dream's reality.

Commit to that vision.

Plant yourself into the soil of your dream.

Water it with sacrifice.

Weed it with discipline.

Let the sun of patience and perseverance shine upon it.

Be so immersed in your dream that quitting is no longer an option.

Give it your life.

If you must, bleed for it.

Endure the nights.

Embrace the silence.

Stay through the slow seasons.

Celebrate the small wins.

And above all—*do not stop until you see fruit.*

This is how dreams become movements.

This is how visionaries become history-makers.

This is how legacies are built.

This is how Heaven kisses Earth—when people obey God's whispers with grit and tenacity.

Do you believe your dream can happen?

If yes, then what's stopping you?

If you believe, If *I* believe, If *God* believes—Then three witnesses have already confirmed it. That's more than enough.

So stop sleeping on it.

Stop rehearsing it in your head.

Start walking. Start building.

And don't stop until you've made the invisible visible.

Your dream is waiting for your action.

I believe in you.

Day 20
CREATED TO BE A BLESSING

"We feel our greatest achievements of success not when we accomplish something for ourselves. We feel our greatest achievements of success when we enable others to accomplish a goal that matters to them"

- Simon Nilek

Listen—when your entire life is wrapped around *you*, you cannot fulfill your purpose. Yes, you matter. You're important. But so are the people around you. You were not created just to enjoy life for yourself, your family, or your close friends. You were created to *bless the world*. You are a vessel of impact waiting to be poured out.

Look at Jesus—He didn't live and die just to bless His immediate circle. He gave Himself for the entire world—past, present, and future. His sacrifice has transformed generations.

Apostle Paul was the same. He poured himself out for the sake of others. Centuries later, we still read his letters, quote his insights, and live by the truths he gave his life for.

Now ask yourself: *Who will be blessed because I lived?*

You can't afford to live selfishly. Your life is not your own—it was bought with a price and designed for a purpose far greater than comfort or self-preservation. If you've been holding back—hiding your gifts, delaying your service, minimizing your contribution—it's time to stop.

Stop holding back.

Stop thinking small.

Stop making excuses.

Start living with open hands and an open heart. You were *meant* to bless your generation.

This doesn't mean you ignore your needs. It's not about burnout or constant sacrifice. It's about breaking free from *self-obsession* and recognizing that real joy, fulfilment, and purpose are found in *giving*, not just receiving.

"It is more blessed to give than to receive."
— Acts 20:35

Think of the lives of men like Bishop David Oyedepo and Pastor E.A. Adeboye. As of the time of writing this, their impact stretches across nations. They didn't become generational blessings by living for themselves. They surrendered their gifts for God's glory and the good of others—and the ripple effect will continue long after they're gone.

One of the greatest secrets to fulfilling purpose is to *help people with what you've been given*. God has blessed every one of us with *something*. Nobody is empty. Your voice, your story, your perspective, your talent, your time—these are gifts. They may seem small to you, but in God's hands, they are seeds of greatness.

And here's a truth you must hold onto:

Everything you have was given to you.

Nothing you carry is random.

Nothing you own is purely for you.

It was *entrusted* to you so that you could bless others.

"What do you have that you did not receive?"

— 1 Corinthians 4:7

Your resources, your influence, your money, your experience, your passion—they were all given so you could maximize them to make someone else's life better. You are not a cul-de-sac. You are a channel.

You were built to give and receive. But if you truly want to walk in a life of purpose and influence, you must seek to *give more than you receive*. That's where the power is. When you live open-handed, heaven responds.

The true blessing isn't in the getting. It's in the *giving*.

If you want to be blessed, *be a blessing*.

If you want to receive more, *give more*.

If you want to walk in purpose, *serve purposefully*.

Your gifts will multiply as you pour them out.

Every single day, wake up and ask yourself:

How can I be a blessing today?

That one question can change your posture. It will stretch your heart, sharpen your purpose, and unlock your joy.

And what will happen when you live this way?

You'll feel fulfilled.

You'll feel alive.

You'll feel grounded.

You'll feel deeply *on mission*—because you are.

This is the life you were made for.

To bless.

To serve.

To impact.

To shine.

This is your mission.

This is your assignment.

This is your calling.

This is purpose.

This is life.

Don't wait another day.

Live for more than yourself.

Live for *others*.

Live for *eternity*.

Live on *purpose*.

I believe in you.

Day 21
A LITTLE BIT MORE

I had just failed a major exam in high school. I was devastated, ashamed, frustrated, and exhausted from what I *thought* was my best effort.

As I sulked, one of my teachers called me aside. I showed him my result with trembling hands, expecting pity or empty consolation. Instead, he looked me straight in the eye and said:

"You are like a boxer in the ring. You're throwing punches, but they're not strong enough to bring your opponent down. He's rocking side to side, front to back but he's not falling. You've got to punch harder. Keep punching until he hits the ground."

At first, I didn't know how to respond. But as I walked away, something in me snapped not in defeat, but in *resolve*. I wasn't angry at the teacher. I was angry at failure. And more importantly, I was ready to fight.

That year, I made a decision. I would give it everything. I slept less. Studied more. Took extra classes. I surrounded myself with determined people. I became laser-focused. And guess what?

I passed. With flying colours.

What changed?

I didn't gain new magic overnight.

I just **punched harder**. I pressed deeper. I gave more.

Maybe you're reading this and you're wondering why, despite all your effort, things still aren't working. You're:

- Asking, but getting no answers
- Seeking, but finding nothing
- Knocking, but the doors remain closed

Let me encourage you:

Don't stop asking—ask again!

Don't quit seeking—seek deeper!

Don't stop knocking—pound on that door until it opens!

You're not throwing punches in vain.

You're *softening the walls of resistance*.

You're *testing the strength of your own will*.

You're *training for victory*.

There is a ladder ahead of you—keep climbing.

There is a destiny calling—keep pressing.

Winners don't stop when it's hard; they stop when it's done.

Remember this:

God has already given you **everything you need** for life and purpose (2 Peter 1:3). The ball is in your court. Whether you rise or retreat is now up to you.

Success often requires **one more push**.

One more try.

One more prayer.

One more email.

One more audition.

One more "yes" after a thousand "no's".

Don't stop because of temporary defeat.

Don't give up because of one closed door.

Don't abandon your purpose because of today's pain.

Think about Joseph: betrayed, enslaved, falsely accused, thrown in prison—and yet, even in prison, he *interpreted dreams*! He kept using his gift. He didn't stop *punching*. And in time, he went from prison to the palace.

That's how God works:

He takes the persistence of the faithful and turns it into elevation.

He takes the pain of delay and refines your destiny.

You're not defeated—you're developing.

You're not abandoned—you're being prepared.

So try again.

Write that exam again.

Make that call again.

Believe in that dream again.

Because you are more than a conqueror (Romans 8:37).

You're not built for failure—you're built for *victory*.

And now is not the time to quit.

Now is the time to punch harder.

Because success is waiting…

And it's got *your name* on it.

I believe in you!

Day 22
NOBODY HAS A PERFECT LIFE

I'll never forget meeting Reinhard Bonnke in Singapore in 2007. During our encounter, he shared something that marked me deeply.

He said, *"One day, a young man came to me and said, 'I'd love to be like you. I'd love to preach like you. I'd love to be successful like you.' And I told him, 'You will be if you can carry the burdens I have carried too.'"*

That one statement carried a thousand truths. Because, you see, success doesn't come without scars. It doesn't come without sacrifice. It certainly doesn't come to those who only admire from a distance but are unwilling to embrace the weight behind the glory.

The truth is, successful people are not without problems. As a matter of fact, they often have more problems than most. The only difference is that they've learned to endure. They've learned to carry their cross. They've learned how to navigate life's punches and keep moving. They don't have perfect lives, they just refused to quit.

Show me a person who's doing well, and I'll show you someone who's had to fight through discouragement, rejection, loss, and adversity. That smiling face you admire today once wept in the night. That confident voice you listen to today once trembled in fear. That giant in the faith you celebrate today once wrestled with self-doubt, sin, and brokenness.

So if you think God can't use you because of your imperfections, you're believing a lie.

Moses stuttered and gave excuses but God still used him to part the Red Sea.

Paul was a persecutor, a murderer of Christians but God turned him into an apostle, and he went on to write most of the New Testament.

The woman with the issue of blood had been bleeding for twelve years, broke and broken—but God healed her, and her testimony still inspires us today.

These were not flawless people. They were just *available* people. God doesn't call the perfect; He perfects the called.

That flaw you're trying to hide might just be the platform God wants to use to showcase His glory.

That pain you've endured may be the very message someone else needs to hear.

That dark season may be the soil in which God is planting something eternal.

Nobody has it all together.

Not the preacher.

Not the influencer.

Not the power couple on Instagram.

Not even your role model. Everyone has something they're battling. So instead of comparing or wishing for someone else's life, tend to yours.

You see someone smiling in church; what you don't see is the silent battle they fought to even show up.

You see a woman dressed beautifully on social media—what you don't see is the loneliness or heartbreak hidden behind the smile.

You admire that man who seems to have it all together—but you don't see the spiritual warfare he fights when the lights go off.

So be careful what you envy. You may want their story, but can you handle their struggles? Can you carry their burdens?

The truth is, your life is enough.

It may not be glamorous.

It may not look like much right now.

But in God's hands, your life is more than enough.

You don't need to be born into wealth to make impact.

You don't need a million followers to be significant.

You don't need a spotless record to be used by God.

You just need to say, *"Here I am, Lord. Use me."*

Because the grass will never look greener on the other side if you're too busy watering yours. And that's exactly what you should be doing—watering your own ground.

So what if your story includes pain? God rewrites stories.

So what if your path has been filled with detours? God redeems time.

So what if your past is messy? God specialises in messes—He turns them into messages.

Stop hiding. Start healing. Stop comparing. Start growing.

God is not looking for perfection—He's looking for surrender.

And guess what? He hasn't given up on you. So don't you dare give up on yourself.

I believe in you.

Day 23
GO FOR IT!

Have you made enough mistakes yet?

Have you allowed yourself the grace to stumble, to get it wrong, to be messy in the process of becoming excellent?

Because you'll never become great by spectating. You won't rise by sitting back and admiring those who've put in the work while you remain idle. Greatness doesn't happen in the shadows of hesitation. You don't become a great speaker just by watching other speakers on YouTube. You don't become a world-class musician by replaying someone else's tracks on your playlist. You don't become a voice to your generation by locking yourself in and hiding behind fear.

You must step into the arena.

Destiny is not for the passive. It's for those who dare. Those who get on the field. Those who risk being misunderstood, criticised, even mocked—just to honour what God has placed within them.

You must try and fail, then try again and fail better. That's how growth happens. That's how mastery is formed. Excellence isn't born in a day; it is forged through discomfort, sweat, humility, and repetition.

Practice. Practice. Practice.

John Maxwell once said, *"Successful people practice harder and longer than unsuccessful people."* That's it right there. The difference isn't always in talent many have talent. But those who rise are those who put their talent to work. Hard work. Focused effort. Relentless commitment.

Stop waiting for destiny to find you. Destiny responds to movement. It meets you *on the go.* Even the woman with the issue of blood didn't wait for healing to come to her bedside. She pushed through the crowd. She made contact with the hem of glory. She *moved.*

And you must move too.

You cannot become great in hiding. You cannot live as the light of the world while staying confined to your bedroom. Jesus Himself said, *"You are the light of the world"*—not the *light of your couch, or your insecurities, or your inner circle. You are the light of the world.*

That means the world needs to see you.

Your ideas.

Your gift.

Your voice.

Your work.

Your purpose in motion.

There's a moment recorded in John 7:3–4 that echoes this exact truth. Jesus' brothers said to Him:

"Leave here and go to Judea, so that Your disciples there may see the works You are doing. For no one who wants to be known publicly acts in secret. Since You are doing these things, show Yourself to the world."

Let those last words ring in your heart: "Show yourself to the world."

Now, of course, Jesus replied that His time hadn't yet come and that's a key lesson in discernment. You don't rush ahead of your timing. But once your season is here, once preparation has been made you owe it to God, to yourself, and to the world to show up.

So if your time is now, what are you still waiting for?

Don't sit on your dreams. Don't hide your talent. Don't bury your gifts in the name of humility or fear. If no one is giving you a platform, create one. If you must take a course, take it. If you need to be coached, pay the price. If you need a mentor, pursue one. If you need to build a brand, learn the principles. Do what it takes.

Because what you carry matters.

You were not made to blend in. You were made to shine.

You were not made to shrink back. You were made to stand tall.

You were not made to remain hidden. You were made to manifest.

The world is waiting.

And heaven is cheering.

So come out. Step up. Be seen. Be known. Be heard. Show yourself to the world.

I believe in you.

Day 24
DONT LOSE EVERYTHING!!!

In this chapter, I want to speak to you about something dangerously subtle, something that often goes undetected until its damage is deep and difficult to reverse. I'm talking about pride.

Pride is like a silent cancer of the soul. It creeps in slowly, quietly, under the guise of confidence, competence, or even spirituality. But its effects are devastating. It doesn't need a loud entrance to make a mess. It just needs a little space in your heart—unnoticed, unchecked—and before long, it begins to poison everything precious: your relationships, your peace, your sense of purpose, and ultimately, your walk with God.

The Bible could not be clearer about its danger:

"Pride goes before destruction, and a haughty spirit before a fall." – Proverbs 16:18 This is not just a poetic line. It's a spiritual law. Wherever pride is tolerated, destruction is inevitable. It may not be immediate, but it is certain.

One of the most dangerous aspects of pride is that it often masquerades as something good. It can look like self-confidence, ambition, or boldness. But in its essence, pride is self-exaltation. It says, "I know better than others. I don't need help. I can figure it out myself." At its core, pride is a declaration of independence from God. And that is why it is so dangerous. Pride is anti-God in nature.

The fall of Lucifer in Isaiah 14 is perhaps the clearest illustration of this. Once an archangel in heaven, full of beauty and wisdom, he became consumed with pride. "I will ascend above the heights of the clouds, I will be like the Most High," he said. But God cast him down. Why? Because heaven has no place for pride.

"God resists the proud, but gives grace to the humble." – James 4:6

When you allow pride to rule your heart, you place yourself in opposition to God. He literally sets Himself against the proud. That word "resists" in the Greek implies a military term, as though God takes a battle stance against prideful people. That should deeply sober us.

Pride has destroyed marriages. A wife too proud to submit, a husband too arrogant to listen. Pride has destroyed ministries—leaders who refused correction or accountability. Pride has destroyed friendships, families, businesses, even entire nations. Pride is toxic. And the worst part is, many prideful people don't even realise they are proud.

Ask yourself, how do you respond to correction? Do you always have to be right? Do you struggle to say, "I was wrong"? Are you open to advice, or do you push back immediately? These are not small matters. These are the indicators of whether or not pride has found a home in your heart.

"The way of a fool is right in his own eyes, but a wise man listens to advice." – Proverbs 12:15

Wisdom and pride don't live in the same house. The moment you think you have all the answers, you're already walking the path of destruction. True greatness requires teachability.

Let me show you a contrast through the life of Jesus. Though He was the Son of God, He walked in total humility.

"...He humbled Himself by becoming obedient to the point of death—even death on a cross." – Philippians 2:8

This is God in the flesh, kneeling to wash His disciples' feet. Serving the very people who would betray, deny, and abandon Him. That is the model of humility we are called to follow.

Pride whispers, "Serve me." Humility asks, "How can I serve you?" Pride says, "I deserve this." Humility says, "Everything I have is a gift from God." Pride isolates. Humility connects.

So, what does pride really look like? It's often in our subtle reactions—the inability to take feedback, the need to win every argument, the disdain for correction, the resentment when others succeed, the obsession with status, image, or praise. It's in comparison and competition, in criticism and control. Pride builds walls. Humility builds bridges.

And here is the truth: pride will rob you. It will steal your joy, delay your destiny, hinder your growth, and break the heart of God. Pride is why some people are stuck. Not because they are not gifted or talented, but because they have elevated themselves to a place where no one can reach them—not even God.

But there is hope. The cure for pride is humility. And humility is not thinking less of yourself; it is thinking of yourself less.

It is understanding that all you have is from God, and all you ever will be is by His grace.

Do you want more grace?

Walk in humility.

Do you want open doors?

Check your attitude.

Do you want restoration?

Choose repentance.

God is not looking for perfect people. He's looking for humble people. People who are quick to say, "Lord, I need You." People who will fall on their knees before they fall on their faces. People who will submit their plans, their pride, and their preferences at the foot of the cross.

I want to encourage you today to do a heart check. Ask the Holy Spirit to search your heart. "Search me, O God, and know my heart; test me and know my anxious thoughts." – Psalm 139:23

Invite Him to expose any hidden pride. Ask for the grace to walk in humility. Keep mentors and godly counsel in your life. Stay teachable. Surround yourself with people who can correct you in love.

Don't let pride rob you of what God has prepared for you. Don't miss your assignment because you're too proud to ask for directions. Don't lose your relationships because you're too stubborn to say "I'm sorry." Don't block God's grace with pride—there's far too much at stake.

If you're going to walk in your calling, if you're going to step into your destiny, you must leave pride behind. Heaven is not built on self-promotion. It is built on surrender.

I'll end with this reminder: "Humble yourselves before the Lord, and He will lift you up." – James 4:10

That is God's promise. If you go low, He will raise you high.

I believe in you.

Day 25
PRAY BUT ALSO WORK!

I remember a young man back in my undergraduate days at the university who stood out from the rest—not because of his grades or social presence, but because of his passionate commitment to prayer. He was, without question, the most prayerful person I had ever met. He spent days fasting, often choosing to skip meals and isolate himself on prayer mountains or in quiet corners, fervently seeking God. He attended outreaches more than he did lectures. While others were in classrooms taking notes, he was on his knees interceding. His zeal was admirable, but there was a gap.

This young man had unintentionally embraced a mindset common among many well-meaning Christians: the belief that spiritual activity alone, divorced from diligence and responsibility, is the key to success. While he was praying, he was missing classes. While he was fasting, he was failing academically. He trusted God to show up in exams he didn't prepare for, hoping that favour would fill the gap that study should have covered. But that is not how God works.

Paul, writing to Timothy, made a profound statement that should shape our Christian approach to life:

"This is why we work hard and continue to struggle, for our hope is in the living God, who is the Saviour of all people and particularly of all believers." – 1 Timothy 4:10 (NLT)

Take note of that first phrase: "we work hard." Paul, a man of deep spiritual encounters, divine visions, and miraculous anointing, was also a tireless worker. He travelled long distances on foot, wrote letters under pressure, built tents for income, and preached with such energy that he once continued until someone fell asleep and dropped from a window (Acts 20:9). This was a man who prayed and worked—he did not substitute one for the other.

As believers, we must recognize that trusting God and working hard are not mutually exclusive. In fact, true faith inspires diligence. Trusting God should lead us to take responsibility, not abandon it. We don't work instead of praying, and we don't pray instead of working. We do both intensely.

"Faith without works is dead." – James 2:26

This principle is foundational. You cannot claim to believe God for provision while refusing to sow, serve, build, or plan. You cannot trust God for financial breakthrough while ignoring opportunities to develop your skills or manage resources wisely. God answers prayer, but He also honours principles. One such principle is the value of labour.

"Work hard and become a leader; be lazy and become a slave." – Proverbs 12:24 (NLT)

Laziness is not just a character flaw—it is spiritual negligence. It is a refusal to partner with God for the manifestation of His promises. Many believers today spiritualize their indifference. They call their inactivity "waiting on the Lord" when in truth, they are avoiding responsibility.

God has already given us "all things that pertain to life and godliness" (2 Peter 1:3). That means your talents, your time, your mind, your energy; these are divine resources entrusted to you for a purpose. If you neglect to use them, you're not waiting on God, God is waiting on you.

Even in the Garden of Eden, before sin entered the world, Adam was given work. God placed him in the garden "to tend and keep it" (Genesis 2:15). Work is not a curse, it is a blessing, a calling. God created us to contribute, to build, to cultivate, to lead. The highest heavens belong to God, but the earth He has given to the sons of men (Psalm 115:16). That means we have a responsibility here.

If you're praying for success in your studies, also study. If you're praying for a job, prepare your resume, network, apply. If you're trusting God for a business breakthrough, research, plan, and execute. Miracles are often hidden in mundane obedience.

Let me be clear: there is no spiritual substitute for hard work. You cannot fast your way into skills. You cannot "tongue-talk" your way into excellence. Prayer positions you, but hard work progresses you. Grace opens the door, but effort walks you through it.

There is a dangerous teaching that suggests believers should never struggle or strive. But Paul says, "we work hard and continue to struggle." This is not a contradiction of grace. It is the application of it. Grace is not a license for laziness—it is the divine empowerment to work with purpose and strength.

Jesus Himself, the Son of God, said, "My Father is always working, and so am I." – John 5:17. He healed, taught, walked, served, and sacrificed. The Christian life is a call to both devotion and discipline.

So, what happens when you avoid hard work? You forfeit your influence. You delay your impact. You waste the divine investment placed in you. Every gift you have is a seed, and seeds require cultivation. You must plow, plant, water, and wait.

Whatever you fail to take responsibility for will remain outside your reach. If you neglect your health, your body will reflect it. If you ignore your finances, your bank account will tell the story. If you abandon your calling, someone else will fill that gap, and purpose will find another willing vessel.

Take a moment and think: are you working as hard as you are praying? Are you putting in the hours, the discipline, the focus? Are you reading the books, attending the training, sharpening your skills? Or have you been using spirituality to avoid responsibility?

Let me challenge you today: rise above passive Christianity. Don't settle for a life of mediocrity dressed in spiritual language. Get up, get moving, and do the work.

There's a proverb that says, "The lazy man desires, yet has nothing." Desire is not enough. Intentions are not enough. Even fasting, without faithful action, is not enough.

So, pray like everything depends on God, and work like everything depends on you. Trust like a child, but toil like a warrior. Remember, even the promised land required giants to be fought and fields to be tilled. There is no shortcut to the top.

I want you to reach the peak of your destiny. I want you to be excellent, fruitful, and favoured. But above all, I want you to understand this; God honours effort. If you will rise and take responsibility, He will meet you with grace and power.

I believe in you.

Day 26
YOU MUST KNOW WHAT YOU DONT KNOW

It is a dangerous thing not to know what you do not know.

There is an ancient Arabian proverb I came across some years ago that has stuck with me ever since. It reads:

"He who knows not, and knows not that he knows not, is a fool; shun him.

He who knows not, and knows that he knows not, is a student; teach him.

He who knows, and knows not that he knows, is asleep; wake him

He who knows, and knows that he knows, is wise; follow him."

Let us focus on the very first line. The proverb speaks of a person who knows nothing, yet is entirely unaware of their ignorance. It calls such a person a fool. Why? Because this is the most dangerous form of ignorance. It is not just the absence of knowledge, but a hardened heart against learning or change. It is an ignorance that blinds and deafens, making wisdom inaccessible.

This kind of ignorance is not just foolish; it is destructive. The Bible echoes this reality in Hosea 4:6, where God says:

"My people are destroyed for lack of knowledge: because thou hast rejected knowledge, I will also reject thee..."

Take note of the second part of that verse: *"because thou hast rejected knowledge."* This shows us that the issue is not just about lacking knowledge, but deliberately turning away from it. Many people do not suffer from a shortage of information; they suffer because they reject the information that could change their lives. This is not mere ignorance—it is rebellion against truth.

And that rebellion is often wrapped in comfort. It is called complacency. Complacency is a silent destroyer. It tells you, "You've done enough." It lies to you that there is no more to conquer, no more to learn, no more to build. It persuades you that your small achievements are sufficient, and that there is no need to strive for excellence.

But complacency is not contentment. While contentment celebrates God's faithfulness in what you have, complacency denies God's potential in what you could become. It is the mindset that keeps many from fulfilling purpose. It cages greatness within a comfort zone. It convinces the talented singer that rehearsing more is unnecessary. It tells the young leader that reading, growing, and sharpening are optional. But if you are truly committed to your calling, then you must understand that you have not arrived. There is more. Always.

Paul said in Philippians 3:13–14:

"Brethren, I count not myself to have apprehended: but this one thing I do, forgetting those things which are behind, and reaching forth unto those things which are before, I press toward the mark for the prize of the high calling of God in Christ Jesus."

If Paul, the apostle who wrote much of the New Testament, did not count himself to have arrived, then neither should we. A refusal to grow is a rejection of destiny. A refusal to learn is a resistance to transformation.

Let's bring this closer to home.

You know you need to set clear goals. You've heard it over and over again. You know there is a target you should be working toward this quarter, and yet, here you are—still drifting, still postponing, still unbothered. If you continue on this path, the outcome is already certain. At the end of the quarter, you will find yourself with nothing tangible to show. Not because you were cursed. Not because the devil fought you. But because you rejected what you knew you needed to do.

You know you need to read books, yet this year, you have not read one. You know you should attend conferences, workshops, or mentorship programmes, yet you keep pushing them aside. Why? Because it feels costly. Because it demands effort. Because you think you still have time. But time is not waiting. And ignorance is not neutral, it is an enemy. It works silently, but its consequences are loud.

Excuses are another form of silent rebellion. You may have a hundred reasons why you cannot afford the knowledge you need. A hundred justifications for staying where you are. But none of them will build your future. Excuses are tools in the hands of those who have refused to evolve. They sound noble, but they are dangerous. Excuses only exist where vision has become blurred.

Jesus never coddled excuse-makers. In Luke 14, when those invited to the banquet began making excuses, the master of the feast became angry and turned to others. This is a sobering truth: destiny does not wait forever. Opportunities can pass you by when you do not value them.

Let me say it clearly. Whatever you fail to take responsibility for will stay outside your reach. It does not matter how much you pray or how many prophecies you receive. If you do not take responsibility, you will not see results. Whether it is wealth, influence, wisdom, or growth—none of it comes to the irresponsible. Heaven's partnership with man is activated by responsibility.

God has already given you all things that pertain to life and godliness. But He will not do for you what He has given you the power to do. Grace is not a substitute for effort. It is the divine enablement to act, to pursue, to build, and to finish.

You have to make the decision today to stop ignoring what you know. Stop pretending that knowledge will somehow work on your behalf without action. Stop rejecting the wisdom that would have moved you forward.

Proverbs 1:7 says:

"The fear of the Lord is the beginning of knowledge: but fools despise wisdom and instruction."

Let that not be you. Do not despise wisdom. Do not reject learning. Do not be comfortable with what you know now. There is more. Press into it. Seek it. Pay the price for it.

Do not let ignorance rule your life. Chase after growth with urgency. And when you find wisdom, apply it.

Your transformation is tied to the knowledge you're willing to pursue, receive, and act upon.

I believe in you.

Day 27
WHAT IS YOUR GOAL?

Imagine watching a soccer game where both teams refuse to take a shot at goal. You wouldn't sit through the entire 90 minutes, would you? It would be one of the most boring matches ever played. Why? Because the entire essence of any game is in the goals scored. No matter the sport, all eyes are on the goal and the scoreboard. If neither team is taking a shot, then it isn't a game worth watching.

Now, envision your life as a game. Are you taking any shots? Are you aiming at any goals? Or are you playing it safe, staying on the defensive, and refusing to advance?

Many people live life as though they are spectators in their own journey. They get inspired, they dream, they plan, but they never take action. They have brilliant ideas but never launch. They are full of potential but lack motion. As soon as a thought comes, fear sets in:

What if people don't like it? What if it fails? What if I'm not qualified? What if I lose?

These "what ifs" are the roots of mediocrity. They keep people trapped on the sidelines. You never applied for the job because you felt you weren't good enough. You never pursued that opportunity because you thought it wasn't meant for someone like you. You passed up countless doors simply because you had no clear target.

Let me tell you the truth: when you don't know your goal, you won't recognize your opportunity. Life is designed to reward those who aim and take action. If you're not taking shots at life, you'll soon be benched by life itself. The difference between those making impact and those stuck in cycles is this; the ones making impact are not afraid to shoot.

Scripture says in Philippians 3:14, "I press toward the mark for the prize of the high calling of God in Christ Jesus." Paul had a clear goal. He was not aimless. He was not casual about his calling. He pressed. He reached. He pursued. That's how goals are scored — not by wishing, but by pressing.

As you evaluate your life this year, ask yourself: Have you taken any real shots?

How many ideas have you pursued? How many books have you read? How many courses have you enrolled in? Have you taken time to discover your purpose? Have you applied for that promotion or scholarship? Did you set clear, actionable goals for the year?

Or have you stayed on the defensive, protecting your comfort zone, justifying your passivity with excuses?

James 2:17 reminds us, "Faith without works is dead." It's not enough to believe. You must act. Faith must be expressed through works. If you're praying for open doors but not moving your feet, you'll remain where you are.

You cannot conquer what you refuse to confront. Life is not a game to be watched. It's a mission to be lived. God has put something in your hands. He expects you to use it. The parable of the talents in Matthew 25:14–30 is a clear example. The servant who buried his talent was judged, not because he wasted it, but because he did nothing with it.

Stop hiding behind fear. Stop giving yourself reasons not to act. Your greatness is on the other side of your shot. Yes, it might miss. Yes, people might criticize. Yes, you may not get it right the first time. But at least you tried.

In sports, no one scores without attempting. In life, no one advances without moving.

Ecclesiastes 11:4 says, "He who observes the wind will not sow, and he who regards the clouds will not reap." If you keep waiting for perfect conditions, you'll never act. There is no perfect time. Now is the time to shoot your shot.

Think of David. When he faced Goliath, he took a shot. Everyone else was afraid, but David ran toward the giant with what he had — a sling and a stone. One shot changed his life. One bold move opened his destiny. Your shot may just be the key to your next level.

As the year progresses, take a personal audit. Ask yourself, what have I tried? What have I launched? What risk have I taken? What dream have I pursued?

Don't stay on the defensive. Get in the game. Take the shot. Make the move. And trust God to multiply your effort.

The world is not waiting for spectators. It's waiting for doers. Romans 8:19 says, "For the earnest expectation of the creature waiteth for the manifestation of the sons of God." The world is waiting for you to show up, not to sit back.

So this year, don't just talk about your goals — chase them. Don't just dream — act. Don't just plan — pursue. Take the shot.

I believe in you.

Day 28
WHY PEOPLE MAKE THE WRONG DECISIONS

Have you ever wondered why people make wrong decisions? Why we sometimes take steps that, in hindsight, seem foolish or unwise? It's not always because we lack information. Sometimes, we simply fail to involve the One who knows the end from the beginning—God.

In Genesis 12, God clearly instructed Abraham: "Leave your country, your people and your father's household and go to the land I will show you." Abraham obeyed, but not completely. He took his nephew Lot with him, even though God never mentioned taking anyone along. At first glance, it may have seemed harmless. But later, this decision would reveal its consequences.

When Abraham arrived in the land, a famine broke out. Instead of seeking God for the next step, Abraham acted out of logic and self-preservation—he went to Egypt. There is no record that he inquired of the Lord. Egypt looked like a better option at the time, but it wasn't God's idea. And just like that, Abraham began making decisions on his own terms.

This is where many of us fall short. Instead of leaning into God's voice during uncertain times, we lean on our own understanding. Proverbs 3:5–6 reminds us, "Trust in the Lord with all your heart and lean not on your own understanding;

in all your ways submit to Him, and He will make your paths straight."

In Egypt, Abraham compounded his error. Afraid for his life, he asked his wife Sarah to lie and say she was his sister. As a result, Pharaoh took Sarah into his palace. It took divine intervention to preserve her purity and protect Abraham's destiny. God, in His mercy, stepped in to rescue them, but make no mistake—Abraham's choices led them into that danger.

And here's something profound: When Abraham finally left Egypt, he returned to Bethel—the very place he had previously built an altar. It was a return to where he had last encountered God. Genesis 13:3–4 says, "From the Negev, he went from place to place until he came to Bethel...where he had first built an altar. There Abram called on the name of the Lord."

This is a picture of repentance and realignment. When we make poor choices, the way forward is often to go back—to the place where we last heard God. To the altar. To prayer. To surrender. Abraham had gained material wealth in Egypt, but spiritually, he had taken a step back. It wasn't until he returned to Bethel that clarity returned.

Here's the spiritual truth: every wrong decision takes us in circles. Until we align with God's will, we often find ourselves back at square one. God may bless us with mercy and even provision along the way, but the delay and detour cost us time, peace, and often relationships.

In Abraham's case, Lot also acquired wealth in Egypt. And soon after, the land could not contain both of them. Their herdsmen quarreled, and Abraham had to let Lot go his way. This moment set the stage for future conflict and heartache. One decision—taking Lot along—planted seeds of unnecessary tension.

Wrong decisions do not only affect us, they affect everyone connected to us. As believers, our choices carry weight. Every step we take outside of God's counsel has consequences, even if they don't show up immediately.

James 1:5 gives a powerful promise: "If any of you lacks wisdom, let him ask of God, who gives generously to all without finding fault, and it will be given to you." This verse is an open invitation to divine direction. God is not withholding His wisdom. The question is: Are we asking for it?

So why do people make wrong decisions?

1. **Impatience:** We often rush ahead without waiting for God's timing.
2. **Fear:** Like Abraham in Egypt, we act out of fear instead of faith.
3. **Overconfidence:** We think we've figured it out, so we stop consulting God.
4. **Pressure:** External expectations cloud our judgment.
5. **Ignorance of God's Word:** When we don't know what God has said, we don't know how to apply it.

But there's good news. Mistakes don't disqualify us. Abraham's story didn't end in Egypt. He realigned. He returned. And God continued to lead him, bless him, and fulfill His promises.

Friend, don't let one bad choice define you. But also, don't keep repeating the same pattern. Learn from Abraham—return to the altar. Involve God again. Let Him lead your decisions.

Make it your resolve from now on: Never move without God. Let this be your prayer: "Lord, before I take a step, speak.

Before I make a decision, lead. Before I go anywhere, go before me."

Psalm 32:8 declares: "I will instruct you and teach you in the way you should go; I will counsel you with my loving eye on you."

The God who led Abraham is still leading today. But He leads those who listen. Slow down. Seek His face. Then move. And when you move with God, you move in the right direction.

I believe in you.

Day 29
COME OUT AND STEP OUT

Do not be that child of God who hears God's instruction or receives His vision and fails to act on it. There exists a category of believers who regularly hear God, but never take steps in obedience. They treat divine instructions as optional suggestions. Do not be counted among them.

There are those whom God instructed to write a book as far back as 2014, yet to this day, they have not picked up a pen. Others were told to take the message God placed in their hearts to the nations in 2013, and now it is 2025, and they have not even left their neighbourhood. There are believers who have clearly heard God say, "Leave your father's house, leave your country, go to the land I will show you," and yet they remain rooted in the same location, five years later.

Obedience to divine instruction is not optional for the child of God. Faith is not measured by how often you hear God, but by how quickly you act on what He has said. Hebrews 11:8 tells us, "By faith Abraham, when called to go to a place he would later receive as his inheritance, obeyed and went, even though he did not know where he was going." That is what faith looks like. God speaks and you respond, not when it is convenient, but when He says it.

Faith is stepping out when there are no guarantees. It is hearing God's voice in the storm and stepping out of the boat like Peter. Matthew 14:29 says, "Then Peter got down out of the boat, walked on the water and came toward Jesus." That was not just a miracle, it was obedience under pressure, faith in action. Storms did not stop Peter from stepping out. Storms should not stop you either.

When Jesus and His disciples were crossing over to another region, a storm arose on the sea (Mark 4:37). The waves beat against the boat, yet the presence of Jesus ensured the storm would not have the final say. That is your assurance too. Storms may rise when you set out in obedience, but they cannot overcome you when Jesus is in your boat.

Your life's storms are often strategically placed to scare you into passivity. They are not designed to destroy you, but to discourage your progress. Storms know that if you step out, you will change things. Your obedience will bring transformation. You will see results, lives will be changed, and destinies impacted.

Stop living like you have no future. Stop sitting idle when you should be advancing. There are goals to smash, lands to conquer, and souls to reach. You were not created to remain in the boat; you were made to walk on water.

God has equipped you with everything you need for the assignment. Stop waiting until you have all the money or all the support. If God has called you, He will provide for you. He is not a man that He should lie. Philippians 4:13 declares, "I can do all things through Christ who strengthens me." That includes the vision God gave you.

If you think you can, you will. If you think you cannot, you will not. As a man thinks in his heart, so is he (Proverbs 23:7). Think you can. Believe that you can. Confess that you can. Then rise and act.

God is not looking for perfect people; He is looking for obedient ones. When you begin to take steps, even small ones, God will multiply your efforts. He supplies strength for each day. You may not have the whole plan figured out, but take the next right step. One act of obedience can shift your entire life.

Trials may come, tests will arise, but that does not mean you are outside the will of God. In fact, it often confirms that you are right where you should be. Do not let fear paralyze your purpose. Do not let the unknown keep you stagnant. Let your faith in God propel you forward.

So, come out of the boat. Come out of your comfort zone. Come out of the excuses and delays. The Lord is waiting on you to obey. Your destiny is waiting for your action.

Take the vision off the shelf. Pick up the pen. Launch the ministry. Start the business. Relocate if you must. Preach the message. Write the song. Apply for that visa. Begin the course. Take the step. The world is waiting for your obedience.

Romans 8:19 says, "For the creation waits in eager expectation for the children of God to be revealed." That revealing starts with a single step of obedience.

I believe in you.

Day 30
YOU CAN MAKE A DIFFERENCE

Some time ago, one of my old high school mates reached out to me with a heavy heart. He was in a very dark place, overwhelmed by life's challenges and seriously contemplating ending it all. He said he had lost hope. To the glory of God, as I write this today, that same young man is filled with hope and passion. He has found purpose, and he is learning to live a life of significance.

What changed? In the few weeks we spent talking, mentoring, and praying together, something shifted. I helped him see life through a new lens. He began to understand that his life has value, not because of fame, wealth, or popularity, but because of the impact he can make in the lives of others. He discovered that significance is not about applause or recognition, but about service. And I want to share that same truth with you today.

You do not have to be rich to be significant.

You do not have to be famous to live a life that matters.

You do not have to be a celebrity to leave a mark on this world.

To live a life of significance means to make a difference in the lives of others – every single day, wherever you are, with whatever you have.

Let's break that down:

1. **Make a difference daily**: Living significantly is not an occasional act, it is a daily commitment. Jesus said in Matthew 5:16, "Let your light so shine before men, that they may see your good works and glorify your Father in heaven." Every day, God gives you opportunities to shine. It could be through an encouraging word, a helping hand, or a listening ear.
2. **Anywhere you are**: Significance is not tied to a location. You don't need a stage or a spotlight. Joseph served faithfully in Potiphar's house, in prison, and in Pharaoh's palace. In every place, his service made a difference. You can be significant in your home, school, workplace, church, or community. Just be available.
3. **With whatever you have**: God never asks us to give what we don't have. In Exodus 4:2, God asked Moses, "What is that in your hand?" Moses replied, "A rod." That simple staff became the tool for mighty miracles. David had a sling, the widow had a jar of oil, the boy

had five loaves and two fish – and each became a channel for God's power. So what do you have? A gift? A skill? A voice? A kind heart? Use it!

Stop waiting for more. Stop downplaying your gifts. Stop thinking what you have is too small. Begin to use what you have, right where you are, and trust God to multiply it.

You may say, "But I'm not qualified."

Neither was Gideon.

You may say, "I don't have much."

Neither did the widow.

You may say, "I'm too young."

Neither was Jeremiah.

The truth is, God qualifies the willing. If you make yourself available, He will make you impactful. Living a life of significance is not about waiting for the perfect moment, it's about choosing to act now with what God has placed in your hands.

Romans 12:6 reminds us, "Having then gifts differing according to the grace that is given to us, let us use them..."

Everyone making a difference in the world today started somewhere. They didn't all begin with large audiences or grand platforms. Some started in small rooms, with nothing but passion, faith, and a burden for people. Some began with tears in their eyes but fire in their hearts. What matters most is that they started. You too can start today.

The world is waiting for your manifestation. Romans 8:19 says, "For the earnest expectation of the creature waiteth for the manifestation of the sons of God." This means there are lives tied to your obedience. There are destinies linked to your significance. There are people who will never find their way if you don't rise to live the life God has called you to live.

Don't fail your generation.

Don't fail the God who called you.

Don't fail yourself.

Begin now. Start with a conversation. Share a testimony. Write that book. Organize that outreach. Offer a helping hand. Start a Bible study group. Mentor someone. Give a meal. Send that message of encouragement. Pray for that friend. There are countless ways to be significant.

Remember, you were not created to merely exist. You were created to make impact. To reflect Christ. To serve. To love. To lead.

Ephesians 2:10 says, "For we are His workmanship, created in Christ Jesus unto good works, which God hath before ordained that we should walk in them."

You were made for good works. You were designed for significance. And today is a good day to begin.

I believe in you.

www.ingramcontent.com/pod-product-compliance
Lightning Source LLC
LaVergne TN
LVHW091545060526
838200LV00036B/711